ACADIAN

One Family and the Great Expulsion

ACADIAN DRIFTWOOD

TYLER LeBLANC

GOOSE LANE

Edited by Jill Ainsley.
Cover and page design by Julie Scriver.
On the cover: *Lueurs* copyright © 2017 by Raymond Martin, oil on canvas, 27.9x 35.5 cm. (Photographed by Mathieu Leger). Map overlay: *Carte de l'Acadie, Isle Royale, et Païs Voisins : pour servir à l'Histoire Générale des voyages by Jacques Nicolas Bellin, 1703-1772.* (Norman B. Leventhal Map Center, Boston Public Library). Map of Acadia and family tree by Emily Powers.
Printed in Canada.
10 9 8 7 6 5 4 3 2 1

Library and Archives Canada Cataloguing in Publication

Title: Acadian driftwood : one family and the Great Expulsion / Tyler LeBlanc.
Names: LeBlanc, Tyler, 1989- author.
Description: Includes bibliographical references.
Identifiers: Canadiana (print) 20190188030 | Canadiana (ebook) 20190188065 | ISBN 9781773101187 (softcover) | ISBN 9781773101194 (EPUB) | ISBN 9781773101200 (Kindle)
Subjects: LCSH: LeBlanc, Tyler, 1989-—Family. | LCSH: Leblanc family. | LCSH: Acadians—Nova Scotia—History—Expulsion, 1755.
Classification: LCC CS90.L4 L43 2020 | DDC 929.20971—dc23

Goose Lane Editions acknowledges the generous support of the Government of Canada, the Canada Council for the Arts, and the Government of New Brunswick.

Goose Lane Editions
500 Beaverbrook Court, Suite 330
Fredericton, New Brunswick
CANADA E3B 5X4
www.gooselane.com

For my grandfather Bob LeBlanc,
the man whose life sparked my interest in this story.

CONTENTS

PREFACE

This book tells the story of a settler culture that attempted to remove and erase another settler culture from lands that neither had the right to call their own. The story is one small part of a much broader history, covering events that predominantly occurred within Mi'kma'ki, the ancestral and unceded territory of the Mi'kmaq People. This territory is covered by the Peace and Friendship Treaties that the Mi'kmaq, Wəlastəkwiyik (Maliseet), and Passamaquoddy Peoples first signed with the British Crown in 1726. These treaties recognized Mi'kmaq and Wəlastəkwiyik title and established the rules for what was to be an ongoing relationship between Nations. I acknowledge Mi'kma'ki, the land where I live and where this book was written, to be unceded territory.

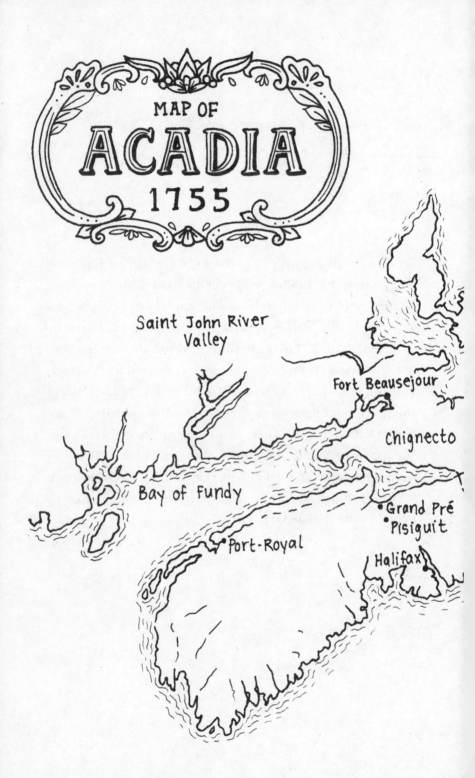

MAP OF
ACADIA
1755

Saint John River
Valley

Fort Beausejour

Chignecto

Bay of Fundy

Grand Pré
Pisiguit

Port-Royal

Halifax

Daniel LeBlanc & Françoise Gaudet
  b. 1626   b. 1623
  d. 1696   d. 1686

René Le Blanc & Anne Bourgeois
  b. 1651   b. 1662
  d. 1734   d. 1747

François Le Blanc & Jeanne Hébert
  b. 1680   b. 1683

- François Le Blanc - b. 1703 d. 1733
- Jacques Le Blanc - b. 1706
- Anne Le Blanc - b. 1708
- Marie Le Blanc - b. 1710
- Joseph Le Blanc - b. 1712
- Marguerite Le Blanc - b. 1714
- Honoré Le Blanc - b. 1716
- Cécile Le Blanc - b. 1717
- Josette Le Blanc - b. 1720
- Madeleine Le Blanc b. 1722
- Jean Baptiste Le Blanc - b. 1725
- Bénoni Le Blanc - b. 1729

Family Tree

1755

PRINCIPAL CHARACTERS

The LeBlancs

François and Jeanne: the parents, living in Pisiguit at the time of the Expulsion

Their Children, in Chronological Order

Jacques: son, married to Catherine Landry, father of seven, living in Pisiguit

Anne: daughter, married to Germain Landry, mother of ten, living in Grand Pré

Marie: daughter, married to Jean Baptiste Thibodeau dit Cramatte, mother of twelve, living in Acadie Française

Joseph: son, married to Marie Josèphe Bourg, father of seven, living on Île Saint-Jean

Marguerite: daughter, married to Charles Hébert, mother of five, living on Île Saint-Jean

Cécile: daughter, married to Charles Landry, mother of six, living in Grand Pré

Josette: daughter, married to Jean Baptiste Landry dit Labbé, mother of ten, living in Riviére des Habitants, Île Royale

Madeleine: daughter, married to Amand Breau, mother of nine, living in Grand Pré

Jean Baptiste: son, married to Marie Landry, father of seven, living in Grand Pré

Bénoni: son, married to Marguerite Hébert, father of three, living in Grand Pré

The Acadians

Joseph Godin dit Bellefontaine dit Beausejour: interpreter and militia leader in the Saint John River Valley

Joseph Broussard dit Beausoleil: militia leader

The French

Charles Deschamps de Boishébert et de Raffetot: military officer and militia leader

Jacques Girard: parish priest at Cobeguit and Saint-Paul-de-la-Pointe-Prime and the sole documented Acadian survivor of the sinking of the *Duke William*

Jean-Louis Le Loutre: missionary priest and militia leader in the Chignecto region

The British

Jeffery Amherst: military commander in charge of the Île Saint-Jean and Île Royale deportations

Robert Dinwiddie: governor of Virginia

Charles Lawrence: lieutenant governor of Nova Scotia; ordered the Expulsion in 1755

Robert Monckton: military commander in charge of the Chignecto deportations

Robert Hunter Morris: governor of Pennsylvania

William Shirley: governor of the Province of Massachusetts Bay

John Winslow: military commander in charge of the Grand Pré deportations

INTRODUCTION

The village of Grand Pré sat between two time-worn Appalachian ridgelines, an undulating land of salt-whitened marsh, plots of sunburnt grain fields, and broadleaf fruit trees. Roughly thirty-seven miles as the crow flies from the scrawny pine lands and wet green-grey granite of the Atlantic shoreline, the wide valley made its own weather, warmer than the coast in summer, drier in winter, and always a little less salty. Life here turned with the heavy tides of the Bay of Fundy. Small homes of one or two rooms, sparsely furnished with softwood chairs and tables and low bunks, where beets, onions, and cabbage simmered in cast-iron pots, lined the area's rivers. Most properties included barns and fields for pasture and crops. Families were large: between eight and twenty-five people could live together. Grand Pré was the hub of a thriving colony, unlike any other on the eastern seaboard of North America.

After more than one hundred years of successful settlement across a tract of land that spread over the modern-day Canadian provinces of Nova Scotia, New Brunswick, and Prince Edward Island and parts of the American state of Maine, the French-speaking settlers who called this place home had become a distinct people situated on the edge of what was quickly

becoming the largest imperial battlefield of their time. Their
realm was known as Acadia (*Acadie* in French) — which linguists
believe to be either a corruption of the word *Arcadia*, a name
given to the region by a seventeenth-century Portuguese map-
maker after the eponymous Greek territory, or the place-name
suffix *cadie*, borrowed from the Mi'kmaq language — and they
were Acadians. They had forged positive relationships with the
Indigenous People who had called the land home for thousands
of years. Allies in battle, and friends and traders in times of
peace, the two groups coexisted in greater harmony than nearly
any other settler-Indigenous cultural interaction of the time.

But Acadia sat strategically positioned on the Atlantic coast,
a highly sought-after piece of territory for Britain and France.
The British had settled around what is now Nova Scotia's capital
city of Halifax in the middle of the eighteenth century and were
set on taking control of the entire area. War seemed inevitable.
The Acadian and Indigenous populations dramatically
outnumbered the British, who both feared and assumed that
the Acadians and their allies would side with the French and
quickly destroy the new British outpost. The land was British,
at least on paper, given by the French to the king of England
during the settlement of a war earlier in the century. Because of
this legal ownership, and in response to the fear of an Acadian
uprising against them, colonial administrators drafted a plan
to remove all the French-speaking colonists — and waited for
the opportune time to implement it. Toward the end of the
hot summer days of 1755, the chance presented itself. After a
brief battle on the border between Nova Scotia and New France
(stretching from today's Newfoundland to the Mississippi
valley), Charles Lawrence, the then lieutenant-governor of the

British colony of Nova Scotia, set in motion a great crime against humanity, the after-effects of which are still felt today.

The village of Grand Pré now exists only as a national historic site, a steel and glass homage to the terrible event that took place over 260 years ago. Nestled in the heart of Nova Scotia's agricultural Annapolis Valley, the site is a popular tourist destination that draws visitors from all over the world. I had been to Grand Pré many times in the years I spent growing up in Nova Scotia. Several of the families affected during the Great Expulsion were my distant ancestors, although I didn't know this until very recently.

During my early twenties I worked as a bicycle tour guide for a Nova Scotia company. One of our most popular trips saw cyclists tour the province's South Shore before looping north toward the Bay of Fundy and eventually ending up in the small town of Wolfville, just a few kilometres down the road from Grand Pré. The final day of the trip included a visit to the site, where guests would tour the grounds, watch a short film, and peruse the museum's small but informative exhibits. While they did this, I would prepare a gourmet picnic for them to enjoy in an adjacent field, after they had finished wandering.

Schedules were tight, and in order to pull off the picnic, which was intended to support the Acadian theme of the day's exploration and usually consisted of francophone-inspired petit déjeuner—croissants, jams, fresh fruit, whipped cream, cured meats, soft cheese, and strong coffee sourced from the local farmers' market—I rarely had the time to actually explore the grounds, read the placards, or enter the memorial church built near the foundations of the original centre of the former Acadian parish. I was there to work, not learn.

The staff at the museum took care of teaching my guests the local history, so I spent less time learning about the Expulsion of the Acadians—the event the site recognizes—than any other component of the trip. After all, this trip was one of ten or more I had to guide each summer in places all over the world, from my backyard in Nova Scotia, to the high mountains of Albania, the archipelagos of western Finland, the sun-drenched hills of Catalonia, Ireland's peat bogs, and many places in between. It was a lot to remember each summer, and since I thought I wasn't Acadian, I figured I'd leave that part of the trip to the experts.

Had I walked with my groups through the grounds, under the sweeping willow trees and across the Kentucky bluegrass lawns dotted with fragrant roses and slender apple trees, entered the memorial church, and flipped through the list of names of those who were called to the church on the day the Expulsion began in the community, I would have found my last name repeated, time after time, scrolled in the delicate ink of a colonial scribe. The names would have meant nothing to me then but may have sparked some form of inquiry.

But I didn't. For years I skipped the tour, more focused on keeping the Brie in my bag cool for the eventual picnic. And I would have likely kept skipping the tour had it not been for a fateful night several summers later. Again I was guiding a bike tour, this time around the famous Cabot Trail on Cape Breton Island. My co-guide, a local of great knowledge, humour, and physical capability, revealed to me my connection to Grand Pré and showed me the path that eventually led to the creation of this book. His name was Michel Aucoin, a wiry grey-haired man from the community of Chéticamp on the northwestern coast of Cape Breton. He had lived most of his life in Chéticamp, spoke Acadian French as his first language, and had worked as a teacher, a historian, and a musician. After a long day of cycling the windy expanse of road between Margaree Harbour and Chéticamp, we set up camp and got to talking.

I grew up on Nova Scotia's South Shore, where the most common surnames are of Dutch and German descent, in a family that originated in Cape Breton, infamously the land of Scottish and Irish stock. French names weren't uncommon, but I always wondered why mine was different from most around me. No one in the immediate family spoke French, and we had no tangible connection to either Acadian or French culture. What was our backstory?

I once asked my great-aunt Margie about it. She grew up with my grandfather, her brother, in Louisbourg, a small town on the east coast of Cape Breton. The French had built a fortress at Louisbourg in the eighteenth century to protect their claims to the North Atlantic fishery and control the seas that led to the St. Lawrence River and France's two largest imperial towns at the time, Montréal and Québec. Margie told me that we were descended from a French convict who survived a shipwreck, swam to shore, and came to live with a family of LeBlancs. He took their name and never, even on his deathbed, revealed his true identity. The first time I heard this story, it seemed to make sense. It explained well enough why we did not share the culture of our name: we weren't really French, or Acadian; technically, it seemed, we weren't even LeBlancs. Though still confusing and mysterious, the story was fun. It was the only one my family had, and they were sticking to it. I went along with it, reciting it often in my early twenties, revelling in this uniqueness. That is, until Michel asked me a few questions.

During many trips guiding tourists around the Cabot Trail, we would cycle past a graveyard full of LeBlancs in the Margaree Valley. I was curious why so many LeBlancs were buried on this side of the island, far from Louisbourg. When I asked Michel about the graveyard, he in turn asked me what I knew about my name. I told him the story of the anonymous French convict. After listening in the receptive manner of an experienced educator, he politely responded that I might want to do a bit of my own research because, more likely than not, that story was false, and my family was in fact Acadian.

Michel had probably heard many familial tall tales like mine before. Acadians were a minority on Cape Breton Island; families with anglicized Gaelic surnames like Campbell, Buchanan, and MacDonald wielded economic and social power, and many nineteenth- and even twentieth-century Acadian families did what they could to conceal their identities in order to fit in. To be identified as Acadian was to be lower class, less than. Many Acadians who flocked in the early twentieth century to Cape Breton's industrial coal and steel towns, like New Waterford and Sydney Mines, attempted to preserve their culture and language, but they struggled. The people who owned Cape Breton's industry spoke and worked only in English, and given that even today some anglophones assume that people who don't speak English are stupid or lazy (or both), it's easy to imagine that the Acadians encountered suspicion and hostility. To find work, they had to adapt, and often this meant concealing their true identity. Acadian societies founded in these industrial towns gradually became little more than social groups or disbanded entirely, like the New Waterford branch of the Société l'Assomption. Though more than half the population of towns like New Waterford is of Acadian descent, the modern identity and culture of the town is vastly more anglophone than in places like Chéticamp or Île Madame (or Isle Madame as it's known today).

When I took Michel's suggestion to look further into my name, it set in motion a curiosity that plunged me into nearly four years of research and transformed the way I thought about identity, family, and the history of the place I call home.

Thanks to the painstaking work of historians and geneslogists before me, it didn't take me long to trace my family name back to a man and a woman who were among the first groups of settlers to arrive in the middle of the seventeenth century in what was then called Acadia and is now called Nova Scotia. I set out to educate myself about the settlement and the eventual removal of its people. I had learned very little about the subject in school, something that is particularly shocking given the regional proximity, so I started with the published general histories of Acadia. Luckily, many talented and devoted historians had travelled this path before me, and I was able to rely on their published works and the documents they had uncovered and translated to guide me on my journey. When I had a handle on the generally agreed upon timeline and facts, I sought out as many primary sources as I could find, which were not many, at least not from the Acadian perspective. Once I thought I understood the event in total, I needed to find out where I fit into it all. With the help of Stephen A. White of the Université de Moncton, the leading Acadian genealogist in the world, I was able to trace my family back to the original LeBlanc family to land in Acadia in the early seventeenth century. More importantly for the context of this book, I was also able to find my connection to the generation that suffered the worst of the Expulsion years: Joseph LeBlanc, my great-great-great-great-great-great-grandfather.

Joseph was born in 1712 and was forty-three when Charles Lawrence signed the deportation order. In an effort to trace the family's connection to the Expulsion, the premise of this book, I needed to know as much about Joseph's generation as possible. It all came together when I linked my genealogical research with a truly remarkable oral testimony, the declaration of Jean Baptiste LeBlanc, Joseph's younger brother. Sitting by the wood stove one morning at my old house in LaHave, Nova Scotia, waiting for a chunk of wet spruce to finally catch fire, I was flipping through an old library copy of *The Acadians in France* when I came across the declarations. I had been on the hunt for Joseph's story for a while at this point and had only recently made the connection between him and myself. I did not expect on that quiet winter morning to make an important discovery. Tracing my index finger down the long list of declarations made by Landrys, Babins, and Doucets, I found Joseph's name listed under Jean Baptiste's oral testimony. Below and above Joseph were the names of each of his siblings and a brief line or two about their lives. It seemed too good to be true. Everything I was looking for was right here under my finger. I had found Joseph's generation, his siblings, the subjects for this book, all in one place, neatly arranged in a list, awaiting further exploration. The narrow research path I had followed until this point suddenly diverged in a hundred different directions.

On the morning of February 25, 1767, Jean Baptiste walked into a small drafty room in the parish of Bangor, on the island of Belle-Île-en-Mer, off the coast of western France, and sat down on a wooden chair. The damp cold outside clung to his coat, a product of the long walk he had endured to arrive at the meeting on time. He had been called to tell four men who he was and where he was from. They were asking all the Acadians on the island, for they wanted to know their stories. Jean Baptiste had a long story to tell, of how he had ended up on this desolate island, thousands of miles from his home, of the trials he had faced getting here, and of what had been lost on the way. He came ready to share his story, happy that someone was interested in hearing his tale.

When he was settled in his chair, the four men asked him to whom he was related, going as far back as he could remember. They wanted to know about his French ancestors. The men asking were Jean Marie Thébaud, Jacques Marie Choblet, Jacques Fronteaux de Lacloir, and the Abbé Jean-Louis Le Loutre. The first three Jean Baptiste did not know; the French court had sent them. Le Loutre, on the other hand, was an old friend of the Acadians, by reputation if not personally. As a missionary he had worked across Acadia, preaching, lecturing, and teaching both Acadians and the Mi'kmaq. He had fought against the British each time they tried to force the Acadians to pledge allegiance to their king. Le Loutre resisted until the last moment before fleeing the region himself, only to end up a prisoner, locked in a castle on the fortified island of Jersey. After his release, he was partly responsible for securing land for Jean Baptiste and the hundreds of other Acadian exiles on

Belle-Île-en-Mer. And now, he sat before Jean Baptiste, along with the scribes and other men of the cloth, attempting one final act on behalf of his adopted Acadian brethren. He wanted to rewrite history.

The parishes of Acadia had kept detailed records of births, baptisms, weddings, and deaths. These documents represented the traceable and ongoing legacy of the flourishing colony started by just a handful of families in the middle of the seventeenth century. But many of these records were burned, tossed into the sea, or otherwise lost when the British uprooted the fifteen thousand who called Acadia home and sent them to the far reaches of the New World. When Jean Baptiste sat down to tell his tale, Le Loutre and the other men from France were likely unaware of the existence of any surviving records. By collecting declarations from the Acadians on the island of Belle-Île-en-Mer, they were creating a new Acadian historiography.

Jean Baptiste had been on the run for twelve years. First the British had locked him up for the crime of being Acadian, and then they had shipped him from place to place. He had spent the first twenty-nine years of his life thinking little of what exactly the term *Acadian* meant. He was Acadian, he had lived in Acadia, and so did his brothers, sisters, cousins, parents, and grandparents. He was his parents' second youngest child in a close-knit family; ten came before him. His siblings helped raise him. When he was young they all lived together in the parish of Grand Pré, the cultural heart of Acadia. The elders in the community were respected, and families shared histories and lives. Blood, marriage, and community connected them. Grand Pré was a homogenous place in those days. As a young man, Jean Baptiste thought little of his political identity—until he had to.

He told the four men in front of him who he was, who his siblings were, who his parents were, who their parents were, and who their parents were. But with his simple declaration, one that he had to affirm verbally because he did not possess the ability to sign the document, he and every other head of a family on the island that spring created a fundamental piece of Acadian genealogical history. The declarations of Belle-Île-en-Mer, as they're now known, fill a historical gap created by a systematic operation of ethnic cleansing carried out against the Acadian people between 1755 and 1763. From the declarations, historians and genealogists have been able to trace hundreds of families' roots through the darkest chapter of the Acadian experience. They have also allowed me to write this book. Jean Baptiste's declaration provided the list of his siblings, and where they were sent during the Expulsion. François, his oldest brother, died before 1755. Honoré, another brother, is absent from any surviving records after 1755 and likely also died before the deportations. Bénoni, Jacques, Madeleine, Anne, Cécile, and Jean Baptiste himself were all deported to the American colonies. Joseph, Marie, and Josette fled Acadia before 1755, and they moved frequently during the years of the Expulsion, always trying to stay a few steps ahead of the British, ending up in communities spread around the region, but they escaped deportation. Marguerite, who also left Acadia before 1755, found herself among the group deported from Île Saint-Jean three years later in 1758.

From this list of siblings comes the cast of characters for my narrative. The small details Jean Baptiste shared served as the breadcrumbs that led me to the ten different stories that follow on these pages.

In tracing just one family's path through this tragic event, I have had to leave out certain aspects of the Expulsion years that the LeBlancs did not directly experience. Indigenous groups were directly and profoundly affected by the settlers' conflicts. Disease and systemic racial warfare resulted in mass depopulation. And once the Expulsion was over, colonial policies intended to wipe out Indigenous culture remained in place for centuries to come. The challenges that people of Acadian descent faced in the nineteenth and twentieth centuries paled in comparison to what Indigenous Peoples endured, and continue to endure. For a more in-depth look into how the European settlement of the Atlantic region affected these groups (in particular the Mi'kmaq), I highly recommend Daniel N. Paul's *We Were Not the Savages*.

Many books before mine have examined the Expulsion of the Acadians. A lot of accounts written by the "winning" side inaccurately represent the fate of the victims or minimize the trauma of this event. Fortunately, Acadian scholars have attempted to correct the imbalance. Wonderful, more accurate resources exist that detail the settlement of the Acadians in the region, the various paths they followed after the Expulsion, the survival of the culture, the socio-political analysis behind the deportations, and nearly everything in between. Generations of genealogists have carefully mapped the family trees of nearly every Acadian family. All of these sources have been vital to my research, but I want to provide a new angle on the tragedy.

As a longtime fan of reconstructed historical non-fiction and its ability to take readers to the time and place in question and bring history alive, I try in these pages to give the Expulsion a similar treatment. This book looks at the event from the point of view of those who experienced it. It is not a grand history of the Acadian experience. I'm not a historian, and I have no thesis to advance. This is a personal book about ten siblings, all distant ancestors of mine, who found themselves tossed from their quiet pastoral lives into the turbulent world of eighteenth-century geopolitics. My subject is not the men in power and their motivations, although in order to properly follow the LeBlancs through the Expulsion, I occasionally shift my focus to the larger and well-documented events. The Expulsion of the Acadians from their homeland had a direct effect on over fifteen thousand people, yet we know very few of their personal stories.

This is a work of creative non-fiction. At times in these stories I tell, I made educated guesses about how the people felt or responded, but I haven't invented dialogue or characters. Any words set off in quotation marks are taken directly from a letter, diary, book, or other historical document. Because my subjects were ordinary people and not major players in any of the events covered, most of their particular suffering has been lost to history. I've paired information found in various documents to construct the most plausible experience for each of the characters. For example, from Jean Baptiste's declaration we know Anne was sent to Philadelphia in 1755, and from genealogical records we know her children later migrated from Pennsylvania to Louisiana. Likely, Anne spent her time in exile in Philadelphia, and I drew on petitions sent to city officials, correspondence between locals that refer to the Acadians, and other historical sources to recreate Anne's experience as an exile in Philadelphia. (My method is similar to that used by Sebastian Junger in *The Perfect Storm*. We will never know exactly how the fishermen on the *Andrea Gail* died, but Junger concluded they most likely drowned and wrote an elegant, heart-wrenching account of what they would have experienced.) I've chosen this same method to put faces to names in a tragedy too often expressed in cold, impersonal figures.

Through writing this book I have found a connection to a history that was almost snuffed out, at least in my family. Acadian culture has made a remarkable comeback, thanks to those who have dedicated their lives to making sure this story is not forgotten. But I am not the only one who had little to no knowledge of their role in this history or the role they could play in contributing to the body of knowledge that keeps the Acadian identity robust and thriving. Though this narrative is full of pain and suffering, it is a story of survival.

CHAPTER ONE

Bénoni

Daniel LeBlanc and his wife, Françoise Gaudet, arrived in Acadia in the middle of the seventeenth century. They settled in Port-Royal, a small community on the north end of the Annapolis Basin, France's first permanent settlement in North America. France had tried to establish a claim in the New World in 1541, on the shore of what would become known as the St. Lawrence River. Jacques Cartier and later Jean-François de La Rocque, Sieur de Roberval, built a small settlement at Cap-Rouge, a headland near the modern-day city of Québec. For two years, they tried to establish a French presence in the area but could not make it work. Six decades later, Samuel de Champlain, a young cartographer from the port city of La Rochelle, sailed into the Bay of Fundy in 1605. He found an inlet that he claimed could shelter the entire French fleet. On these shores, Port-Royal was founded.

The colony struggled to set down roots. Settlers suffered through harsh winters not at all like those in northern France. Wars an ocean away shuffled the small settlement back and forth between British and French hands for nearly thirty years before any real growth began. The first to arrive found salty soil, dramatic tides, and a short growing season. But they dug in. Raising the first dikes in North America, Daniel and the rest of Port-Royal's pioneers shaped a new community by hand, one isolated, independent, and far from the imperial gaze of the King in Paris.

Two generations later, Daniel's grandson François left Port-Royal. Like his grandfather, François sought new lands and freedom. Following a few families that had left before him, François and his wife, Jeanne Hébert, landed in Les Mines, a quilt of kin-linked communities on the edge of the Minas Basin—the shallow tidal gut of the Bay of Fundy—and made their home near Grand Pré, the largest community. When the Acadians arrived in the Les Mines region in the 1680s, the topography must have reminded them of home. Most came from the salt flats of northwestern France, from Brittany and Poitou.

Twice a day, over a billion tonnes of seawater rushed northeast up the funnel-shaped Bay of Fundy, around Cape Split, and spilled into the shallow Minas Basin. The depth, shape, and location of the bay pushed the surging water fifteen metres above the low tide line. On the surface, the tide came in with grace and ease. Below the surface, the waves pounded through the bay with the force of a category five hurricane. Swirling endlessly through the wash came the full bounty of the sea, and with each lunar push the waves gave vast riches of minerals perfect for agriculture to the land. But the tide ebbed with brutal force, stealing from the land what it deposited just hours earlier. To master this force took ingenuity and hard work.

Never far from the flux of the red-stained basin, the settlers harnessed the plundering tides with dike-building technology passed down by their French ancestors. Their dikes, sometimes ten feet or more in height, blocked the incoming tide with ease and drained the protected land. This last detail was crucial: land could not be farmed without proper drainage. They hollowed logs to form sluices, or aboiteaux, and buried them at the base of the dike. At one end of the aboiteau was a hinged flap. Groundwater and rogue tides drained easily through the aboiteau and back into the sea, while the pressure of an incoming tide held the flap shut, stopping any water from entering. The technology worked well, allowing the community to expand in size and food production capabilities. The dikes were managed collectively, and each member of the community had a role in the construction and upkeep of their local walls. Like a fortress holding off a twice-daily siege, the dikes protected Grand Pré from the force of the sea and enabled the Acadians to settle and raise families.

Before the Acadians arrived, the Mi'kmaq had lived in the region for thousands of years. Moving seasonally between coastal summer communities and winter camps in the interior, they were masters of their maritime environment and thrived, establishing distinct communities in what is now Nova Scotia, New Brunswick, Prince Edward Island, and parts of Quebec.

The Mi'kmaq and Acadians found common ground between their two cultures and prospered together. Using the land nomadically, the Mi'kmaq embraced trade and found open minds among Grand Pré settlers. The Acadians reclaimed land from the sea and intruded little on the ancestral territory of the original population, living together in small familial villages on sprawling farmland and pasture. Marriage between Mi'kmaq and Acadian peoples was allowed, even encouraged, and deepened the bonds between the communities. Families grew quickly and had plenty to eat: pork fat, mutton, curdled milk, whole grains, and fresh fish. Robert Hale, a New Englander who travelled through the region in 1731, was surprised by the quality of the protein-rich, fatty diets of the locals. Once planted, the diked land proved perfect for large-scale agriculture, filling tables with tubers, bitter greens, and brassicas. Hemp and flax flourished and were spun and woven to clothe the communities. Between harvests, men rode the tides chasing shiny green-striped shad and other ocean fish in small single-sail punts. Oxen plowed the fields and windmills ground grain to flour. The many rivers of the flatlands served as roads, allowing villagers to gather together to trade goods and attend religious services, such as marriages, baptisms, and funerals, at the parish church.

The Acadians flourished. From the small handful of settlers who arrived in the early 1680s, the population of Grand Pré had increased fifty-fold to nearly five thousand by 1755. François LeBlanc and Jeanne Hébert raised a large family of six sons and six daughters. Infant and child mortality were markedly lower in Acadia than in Europe, with some figures suggesting that up to 75 per cent of children born to Acadian families survived to adulthood. In France at the time, infant mortality rates of up to 50 per cent were reported. All François and Jeanne's children lived to adulthood. In 1733 their firstborn, named for his father, died at the age of thirty. It's possible that another of their children also died in adulthood and before the Expulsion. Honoré, their seventh child, appears on a baptismal record as the godfather of a child baptized in Grand Pré in 1727, but that is the only record of him. He likely never married and either died before 1755 or, unlike the rest of his family, somehow managed to avoid leaving any record of himself. The rest of François and Jeanne's dozen children grew up, married, and had families of their own.

Despite the steady rhythms of hard-working agricultural life, the people of Grand Pré could not entirely avoid awareness of the conflicts between two competing colonial powers. For nearly 150 years, the British dabbled in the conquest of Acadia. They and the French traded the land the Acadians lived on back and forth like beaver pelts. In 1710 the British stormed Port-Royal; three years later the French ceded the colony to them and Port-Royal became Annapolis Royal. Maps labelled *Acadie* became maps bearing the name *Nova Scotia*.

In 1730 the governor of Nova Scotia, Richard Philipps, asked the Acadians to swear an oath of loyalty to the British Crown. The British presence increased. Red-coated soldiers turned trees into forts, including Fort Edward, built atop a round hill, where the town of Windsor, Nova Scotia, now stands. From the top of the blockhouse, sentries could see the innermost reach of the Minas Basin, where the Avon and St. Croix Rivers empty into the sea. The fort's three shabby wooden buildings were put up in the frontier style inside a four-point, star-shaped palisade. Thin but wide planks made up the walls. Central fireplaces heated the rooms. The small parade was cobbled, and the fort included a small hospital. The lone blockhouse had murder holes, small open slits in the wall large enough to fire from but too small to fire into. The top floor was slightly larger than the bottom, and the overhang featured removable floorboards that could be taken out to allow hot oil and burning coals to be dumped on anyone attempting to storm the fort. But the fort was not designed to handle full-scale warfare. It was an outpost, a symbol of power built on the site of an old Acadian church.

Fort Edward was not the only British stronghold dotting the landscape of Nova Scotia. In 1749, during a push to assert British dominance in Acadian communities and prevent an exodus to surrounding French territories, they built a fort a few miles from Grand Pré, on a low-lying field at the basin's edge. Fort Vieux Logis didn't last long. In the autumn of its first year, a militia made up of Acadians and an alliance of Mi'kmaq, Wəlastəkwiyik, Passamaquoddy, Penobscot, and Abenaki fighters known as the Wabanaki Confederacy, attempted a siege on the fort. In the process they captured nineteen British soldiers, including the commander's son, who were patrolling the area outside of the palisades. With prisoners in tow, the force tried to take the fort but retreated after a week of unsuccessful attacks. Their prisoners were ransomed more than a year later. Though no further attempts were made on the fort, its exposed location led the British to abandon it four years later. They left it to rot in the weather.

But many worried that the British build-up in the region meant something dark and terrible, and only increased the risk of getting caught between warring nations if long-standing tensions finally boiled over. One of François's sons, Joseph, had fled with his wife and her family, the Bourgs, to the deep end of the basin, to a place called Cobeguit. Before 1754, his daughters Josette and Marie had also moved away, to the neighbouring French territories of Île Royale (now Cape Breton Island), and Acadie Française (now the Province of New Brunswick). They were the lucky ones. The mounting fear that many experienced as the British presence in the region increased proved justified not long after Josette and Marie left Acadia. In the early days of June 1755, troop transports from New England, containing a mix of British soldiers and New England militiamen, dropped anchor off the low-lying salt marshes of Tantramar on the Isthmus of Chignecto, the narrow strip of land between the colony of Nova Scotia and New France. Perched on the border, overlooking the bay's churning tidal flux, sat two forts, the British Fort Lawrence and the French Fort Beauséjour. Both were frontier outposts, small fortified stations, neither one capable of mounting any real defence against a siege—which is why the British brought cannons.

To France, Fort Beauséjour was a strategic defence point between Louisbourg on the Atlantic and Québec, far inland to the west. To the English, it was the only thing standing in the way of Britain's full occupation of the Atlantic region. The British were confident that the conquest of Acadia would lead inevitably to their ultimate control of North America. On June 4, they attacked.

Under the command of Robert Monckton, a lieutenant general who would later gain fame as the second-in-command to General James Wolfe during the capture of Québec, 2,300 soldiers crossed the Missaguash River and dug in. The terrain was swampy and flat, but the British worked their way closer and closer to the walls of Fort Beauséjour. Forces of French, Acadian, and Indigenous fighters tried to push back the advancing army, but they were outnumbered by more than four to one. Nine days after they landed, the British were able to position their cannons in range of the fort. Under heavy fire, Beauséjour didn't last long.

The mortar shell tore through the fort's ceiling just as a group of officers sat down for breakfast on the morning of the thirteenth. The blast shook the walls and shredded the soldiers to pieces. Louis Du Pont Duchambon de Vergor, commander of the fort, got to his feet as dust from the explosion filtered past his door through the fort's narrow passageways. Abbé Jean-Louis Le Loutre stood at his side.

Vergor went to his quarters, gathered what he needed, and headed for the base of the fort's flagpole. He carefully tied the white flag on the line and ordered it sent up. The cannons stopped. The gates were unbolted. Vergor returned to his quarters and packed his trunk for the long journey ahead of him. He would be sent back to France. What fate would befall the Acadians who'd stood with him, he did not know.

When news of the victory reached Halifax, by then the British capital of the colony of Nova Scotia, 186 miles away, Lieutenant-Governor Charles Lawrence read the letter carefully, his normally stern face betraying his delight. He'd been waiting for this day. An engraving in the Scottish National Gallery depicts Charles Lawrence as a man of unremarkable appearance. He'd come to political appointment by his sword, the same sword he had plunged into the hearts of young Frenchmen on the muddy battlefield of Fontenoy during the War of the Austrian Succession. Now, in the New World, he administered an important British outpost, a place rife with a stubborn population of supposedly neutral farmers who spoke the language of his enemy.

He first arrived in Nova Scotia eight years earlier, in 1747, and was stationed at the former French stronghold at Louisbourg, which the British had recently captured. After some time in the colony as a military man, Lawrence was promoted to lieutenant-governor in 1754. During his stay he'd become familiar with the Acadians and their allies, the Mi'kmaq. He had no love for either group. He had fought the French his whole life, and he was ardently ethnocentric. Together, the Acadians and Indigenous Peoples vastly outnumbered the small crop of British settlers struggling to claim the harsh frontier for the Crown, and in Lawrence's view, they showed an astounding contempt for British models of authority and class. His administrative predecessors had been too lenient, too flexible, too nice. They'd accepted the Acadians' oath of neutrality and offered them cohabitation in return. In Lawrence's mind, these people were "inveterate Enemies," "ungratefull" and "perfidious," deserving of the "severest treatment." For him, their defence of Fort Beauséjour proved their willingness to take up arms against the British. They were snakes in the grass, and Lawrence, as the de facto ruler of this remote realm, had the power to stamp them out. The fall of Fort Beauséjour and the capture of the small number of Acadians who took part in the fort's defence justified for Lawrence the implementation of a plan that the British colonial authorities had first conceived nearly fifty years earlier.

Lawrence pointed to Fort Beauséjour as an excuse to act, but in reality he had struck the first blow many days before the siege of the fort. Soldiers, acting on Lawrence's order, impounded canoes and firearms across Acadia in the days leading up to the siege. The outraged deputies of the largest communities wrote to Lawrence to express their displeasure: "It is not the gun which an inhabitant possesses, that will induce him to revolt, nor the privation of the same gun that will make him more faithful; but his conscience alone must induce him to maintain his oath." They had not been providing assistance to Beauséjour, and they had no intention of being grouped in with any who had, they argued. Their guns were to protect their livestock and families; their canoes were for fishing and transporting goods across the rivers. Proclaiming innocence, they demanded and expected the immediate return of their personal property.

Lawrence likely anticipated their response, for it gave him yet another opportunity he had been waiting for. In early July 1755, under the guise of benevolent diplomacy, he invited the signatories of the petition to his home in Halifax. They came from Les Mines and Pisiguit to speak on behalf of a large number of Acadians spread around the Bay of Fundy. They protested that they were bound by the oath of neutrality their fathers had sworn, and they themselves had no involvement in the defence of Fort Beauséjour. Or they most likely would have, had they been allowed to speak. Lawrence had no interest in hearing what these men had to say. Because they were all guilty in his estimation, he demanded that each one swear an oath of unwavering allegiance to King George II and defend the British colony against the French.

The deputies said they couldn't swear an oath without first speaking with their communities. They reminded the lieutenant-governor that their neutrality was more than words. They had stayed out of the fray throughout decades of conflict in the region, never, as a group, raising arms against the crimson-coat invaders. The war wasn't their concern: Britain had taken control of their land years earlier, and their lives had changed little. They wanted nothing more than to continue to live as they pleased.

Lawrence's stance was firm: swear the oath or be sent away. The deputies left the room to confer with one another. They returned an hour later, more resolved than before. It was not for them to take an oath on behalf of their entire people, they told Lawrence. They would uphold the old oath signed by their fathers, but they would pledge nothing more. Lawrence sent the deputies away for the night to reconsider, but when they appeared the next morning, they gave him another resounding no.

Lawrence ordered the deputies shackled and sent to the prison on Georges Island, a fortified treeless green bump in the middle of Halifax's harbour. Lawrence called for new deputies. They were offered the same option, and they gave the same answer. No more oaths. They'd rather leave their lands than pledge to fight for the British. Again the deputies were shackled and sent away.

Lawrence knew the Acadians would refuse to accept his terms. What would the oath gain for them? After all, in the face of war, which seemed inevitable, the oath worked doubly against them. If the French came to these lands, the Acadians would have been forced to take up arms against their kin from a common homeland, those who spoke their language and followed the tenets of Catholicism. If they refused, the British would condemn them as traitors. If they fought and were caught by the French, they'd also be considered traitors. Treason drew the harshest punishment under law at the time, and death could be prolonged and excruciating.

Of course they would refuse, and that was exactly the response Lawrence wanted. With Fort Beauéjour captured and his offers of diplomacy rejected, he had what he needed to rid the British colony of the Acadians once and for all. They'd be arrested, imprisoned, and forced onto ships bound for the British colonies in the south. The thousands of British troops would set fire to their homes, barns, and possessions. Their livestock would be slaughtered and their crops razed. A hundred years of hard work and humanity would be erased, and loyal British subjects from New England would take their place. Acadia would die, and from its ashes would rise a strong and British Nova Scotia.

The plan had been under consideration for years. London had continually resisted the idea; past governors always wavered. Removing a population of nearly fifteen thousand people was a major undertaking. Ships would need to be rented, captains and crews paid, and garrisons readied in case of rebellion. Other powers might object to the British plan, in particular the French. War could ensue. Lawrence, however, saw beyond the challenges to an opportunity to make his mark in history. And he seized it.

Once the second group of deputies was put in chains and shuffled from Lawrence's sight, the clerk recording the proceedings took down Lawrence's final instruction: "It would be most proper to send them to be distributed amongst the several colonies on the continent, and that a sufficient number of vessels should be hired with all possible expedition for that purpose." Even now, the words seem almost casual.

Thus, Charles Lawrence threw into motion the great upheaval of the Acadian people.

The Expulsion began, quite deliberately, at Fort Beauséjour, now under the command of Robert Monckton. The fort had been renamed Fort Cumberland in honour of King George II's son William Augustus, Duke of Cumberland, also known as Butcher Cumberland for his role in suppressing a Jacobite uprising in the Scottish Highlands in 1746. On August 10, 1755, Monckton's men rounded up and took prisoner as many Acadian men and boys living near the fort as they could find. Then Monckton ordered his captains to fan out across the Chignecto region to capture every Acadian they encountered and burn every building they found. One group headed to the remote village of Tatamagouche, a small hamlet on the sandy southern bank of the Mer Rouge (now the Northumberland Strait). It was a small community: a few farms, a mill, and a church. On clear days, the cliffs of Île St.-Jean (Prince Edward Island) were visible on the horizon, making the strait feel more like a wide bay. No priest lived here, and the church sat empty most days. But the villagers would gather for Mass even without a priest. On the fringe of Acadia, the people were self-reliant.

Army captain Abijah Willard marched into the village on August 14 and asked the men of the community to gather the next morning to receive his message. Willard's soldiers were thirsty and out of rum. Luckily the villagers had beer on hand. "Beere was given this day, in lieu of rum," he wrote in his journal that night.

In anticipation of what the meeting might bring, the men likely stayed up all night discussing what to do. The British hadn't come to this village in a long time, and they knew that an armed battalion rarely meant good things. Nevertheless, the next morning they showed up as requested. As Willard later recorded, "I told them all they must go with me to Fort Cumberland, and burn all their buildings, which made them look very sober and dejected." To add to the injury, while the men were listening to Willard, his soldiers looted their houses, seizing food and a few "fine guns." Ultimately, the British torched the village and arrested the men. Willard gave their wives and children the option of accompanying their husbands and fathers. That they opted to stay in their burned-out village, he admitted, was "something shocking."

Monckton and his raiding parties captured most of the Acadian population of the Chignecto region that fall. Some were lured into forts and imprisoned; others were arrested in scenes like Willard's ambush of Tatamagouche. The British burned their way through the area. If the soldiers found villages already empty, they burned them anyway. Monckton rounded up nearly fifteen hundred Acadians, stuffed them into ships anchored at sea, and readied the vessels to be sent south. When the time was right, they would rendezvous with other ships under the command of other officers, and all crammed beyond capacity with Acadian men, women, and children, near the mouth of the Minas Basin, the gateway to Grand Pré.

On September 5, 1755, François LeBlanc, his eldest son, Jacques, and 181 other men in Pisiguit were summoned to Fort Edward. Captain Alexander Murray had to deliver a message to them from Lieutenant-Governor Charles Lawrence. As the men gathered, they could see the docks just below the fort, where two large wooden ships, troop transports, had tied up that morning. Most of François's family lived roughly twelve miles away in Grand Pré. He often travelled there to see them. Many of his children had married in the church of Saint-Charles-des-Mines. He could travel to Grand Pré and back in one day if the tides were right. As François headed to Fort Edward that September day, he had no way of knowing that he would never make the trip or see most of his children ever again.

In Grand Pré, François's son Bénoni and his wife, Marguerite, lived as farmers, like most in their community. But when the sun rose above their home on September 5, 1755, no one headed to the fields to harvest, even though the wheat had yellowed and the rye was ready to come in. The day before, British soldiers had told all the men and boys over age ten to meet at the church of Saint-Charles-des-Mines at three o'clock sharp to hear Charles Lawrence's message. Bénoni must have known something was going to happen: two weeks earlier a British colonel had arrived by ship with a regiment of soldiers. They had built a palisade around the church, the site of so many important community events; later, they had built another around the cemetery. The colonel was John Winslow, and he had come from New England to carry out Lawrence's order.

Bénoni probably started his morning leaning on the south side of the house, smoking rough shredded leaves from a clay pipe. Like most men of the era, Bénoni enjoyed tobacco brought from New England by the traders who frequented the Minas Basin. The low morning sun turned whites a soft shade of pink and darkened the turnip greens in the garden. It was a wasted day of harvest, to go to the church and listen to an Englishman spout the king's decree. But he would go. Passing the ripe fields of wheat and reddening apple trees, he made the familiar trip to the church of Saint-Charles-des-Mines, the centre of the parish.

Most of the other men and boys from around the area made the same journey from their homes on the low hillsides to the west and east and along the riversides and deltas of the south and north. They didn't know that the year's apple crop would fall unpicked to rot, that their wheat would spoil and wilt, or that they'd never again sleep in their own beds. The tide pulled away from the muddy banks of Grand Pré that day and came back to a world turned upside down.

The church of Saint-Charles-des-Mines was small and humble. It sat beneath a low hill, one side facing the water. Fruit trees and several young willows adorned the churchyard. Their leaves were not yet drained of their summer colour. Over four hundred men and boys gathered, waiting to learn why John Winslow had summoned them. Most of Bénoni's family was among them: his brother Jean Baptiste; brothers-in-law Charles Landry, Germain Landry, and Amand Breau; uncles and cousins. Left at home, the wives and mothers probably thought this would be like the other times when their men had left home to answer to an Englishman. They had signed oaths before, promising this king or that governor that they wouldn't fight if war came.

The soldiers stationed at the church, their temporary barracks, felt the same sun on their heavy coats and a keen sense of fear and anticipation. The men and boys assembled outnumbered them by more than double, and many more "French neutrals" (as they were often referred to by the British) were at home. The Acadians were not likely to receive the message well.

Bénoni entered the church early, but the small room filled up quickly. It didn't look at all the same as the last time he was here. Winslow had forced the priest to strip the holy place of its meaning and sacrament. Soldiers flanked all the walls, standing at attention in their austere military dress. One plain wooden desk sat in the centre of the room. Once all 418 men and boys had arranged themselves inside the building, the soldiers barred the doors. Winslow stood at the table and commanded the Acadians' full attention. At his side stood an interpreter, possibly Father Landry, the bilingual priest of Saint-Charles-des-Mines, or one of several bilingual Huguenots working with the British at Fort Edward in nearby Pisiguit. The air inside the church was hot. The thick-paned glass in the windows and the heat of nearly five hundred bodies amplified the day-long sun.

John Winslow had the look of a bureaucrat. A plump chin rounded the bottom of his face. A tight starched collar turned his neck into a series of creases. His hair was limp and receding. As a great-grandson of the pilgrim Edward Winslow, an original settler of the Plymouth colony in what would become Massachusetts, he was destined to serve the Crown and follow a life of duty and orders. He rose through the ranks of the British military, and at fifty-two he was chosen to carry out Charles Lawrence's plan for the Acadian people.

"Gentlemen," Winslow began. Then he paused for a moment or two. "You are convened together to hear His Majesty's final resolution to the French inhabitants of this, his province of Nova Scotia." The wooden floor creaked beneath shuffling feet. Winslow held his scroll and waited while his words were interpreted. He continued. "Your lands and tenements, cattle of all kinds, and livestock of all sorts, are forfeited to the Crown with

all other of your effects, save your money and household goods."
He paused again while the interpreter repeated his words in
French. The faces before him grew long. "You yourselves are to
be removed from this, his province," he concluded.

A soldier in the room that day wrote that the men's features
altered beyond expression after hearing the news. Bénoni's face
twisted in anger. Men around him adopted similar masks of
rage as they absorbed Winslow's words. Winslow tried to soothe
their anguish. They'd be treated fairly, he told them. No one
would be hurt. They were prisoners of the British Crown and
would be treated as such. Then he left the room. In his journal
he described the day as one of "great fatigue and trouble." At
Fort Edward, Bénoni's father and brother received the same
message from Captain Murray. Keenly aware of close links
between the two communities and determined to blindside the
Acadians, Winslow and Murray made sure they delivered the
news simultaneously.

Offshore, the ships sat at anchor, their sails furled. Twice a
day with each tide, their oil-soaked hulls pitched skyward and
leaned toward the mud. The basin's water sparkled blue under
the midday sun, became gunmetal grey beneath woollen rain
clouds and lay flat and orange in the late evening. Lawrence,
ever the colonial penny-pincher, sourced the motley fleet
from the dregs of Boston's harbour. Most were sloops, vessels
characterized at the time by a single mast, a fore-and-aft gaffed
mainsail, two or three headsails, and often a square topsail
and a small lower sail. Sloops required far fewer sailors and
were easier to crew than the larger square-rigged three- and
four-mast ships and brigantines more commonly used for long-
distance voyages.

Crudely hewn from heavy timbers, hand-sawn and shaped with adzes and broadaxes, the sloops were small, rough, and lacked any form of comfort, although they had been built to carry human cargo on the order of two persons per tonne (*tonnage* has its etymological roots in an old taxation system for charging dues on wine casks, or tuns). The British had modified the ships, lengthening their cargo holds and splitting them into two or three low-ceilinged decks. The dank holds lacked light and air. The *Elizabeth* registered at ninety tonnes, which to Lawrence meant it could hold 180 prisoners, the *Mary* and *Sarah and Molly* likewise. Everyone would have to wait while additional ships were brought to transport them all. From the churchyard, where Bénoni and the others spent their days under guard, they could see the dull brown vessels riding the horizon. They could be forgiven if they thought the ships looked more like giant coffins bobbing on the waves.

Winslow permitted twenty hostages to leave the church each night to tell their families what had happened and to prepare to quit their lands. Bénoni waited for his turn. He probably assumed that his father, François, and his brother Jacques were suffering under similar imprisonment in Pisiguit. The doors remained barred and a duty of twelve guards circled the church day and night. Several days passed, and nothing changed. The men and boys spent their daylight hours in the churchyard and were herded back inside each night to sleep. Conditions were cramped, and they were hungry. The elders petitioned Winslow to let some men go so they could harvest the fields and work the mill. Disbelieving he would actually deport them all, they wanted to bring in their harvests before it was too late. Winslow refused the request. He ordered the prisoners' families to supply food and clothes as best they could to those detained. Meanwhile, wheat fell over in the wind, and the gristmill stood unworked.

After five days, the soldiers marched all the detainees outside. Winslow feared an uprising. Earlier in the summer, French forces and a large militia of Anishinaabeg fighters decimated General Edward Braddock's attempt to advance the British into the Ohio River Valley. Similar quests into the northeastern hinterlands had also failed. As September dragged on, news from battles elsewhere in the realm soured the already edgy mood of the outnumbered British soldiers. Although Winslow ordered his troops to behave, many looted houses and farms and harassed the Acadians. The troops hated the French and cared little that the Acadians claimed no connection to the king in France. At Fort Edward, Captain Murray worried that further delay in boarding the ships would result in bloodshed. He warned Winslow in a letter that his men would surely kill Acadians, given the chance.

In an endeavour to reduce the perceived threat, Winslow asked Father Landry to tell the men that 150 of the most rancorous younger prisoners would embark on the ships immediately. The chosen men refused to go without their fathers. Winslow, of course, ignored them. He ordered some of his soldiers to restrain the young men's fathers, while others forced the chosen ones toward the sea. Winslow, impatient, grabbed a young man by his shoulders and shoved him in line. The soldiers fastened their bayonets and stepped forward in regimental order. Some of the blades were bowed from age and use, others were rigid and fresh. With steel at their backs and their heads bowed, they inched toward the water's edge, while the men cried and sang.

Winslow singled out another hundred, and his men forced them into the same column. Mothers, wives, and children had gathered to watch the scene. They prayed and wept and reached for loved ones about to be forced onto the small wooden landing crafts. Those men spared from immediate deportation were sent back to the church, but soon enough every one of them would make the same solemn walk to the shoreline.

Soups still boiled on small iron stoves, and gardens were picked of their bounty as in previous Septembers, but families no longer sat down together for meals in their small houses. The women and children carried hot meals of bonny clabber—thickly curdled milk—roasted mutton, shad, bread and molasses, and fresh fruit to the church. Some trekked to the shoreline each day to send food to the unlucky souls locked in the holds of the transport ships floating in the basin. Winslow's troops rounded up the families living in nearby villages to fill the empty beds the prisoners once slept in.

October slammed into the Minas Basin with hard winds and heavy rain, further delaying embarkation. Winslow's nerves finally broke when he learned a group of ship-bound prisoners escaped under the watch of eight armed guards. His soldiers brought ashore François Hébert, whom Winslow named as an abettor to the crime. Carried to his home, Hébert arrived just as the torches took hold of his barn. He watched the house he had raised a large family in give way to the flames. Winslow announced that any friends of those who had escaped would face the same punishment unless the rebellious members turned themselves in.

Charles Lawrence was angry the ships weren't yet filled, but Winslow wanted to keep families together, even though it was a logistical nightmare. Murray cared less. "They will be stowed in bulk," he wrote to Winslow late in October. "Let the consequences be what they will be." It was getting late in the month, and Winslow didn't have enough ships to fit everyone as he'd previously promised.

Slowly the soldiers moved the village aboard. As Grand Pré emptied, settlers from the Atlantic coast—German and Dutch Protestants along with off-duty British soldiers and English settlers—pillaged Acadian homesteads, hoping for abandoned treasure. They burned barns, dug up gardens, and ransacked kitchens, outbuildings, and bedroom trunks. Amidst the chaos, Winslow made note in his journal of the first official casualties of the operation. A group found hiding among the remnants of the former parish took to their horses when a search party spotted them. Two dropped at the first volley of musket fire: one man died on horseback, the other succumbed to his wounds later in the evening.

Among those boarding, Bénoni and his wife had taken what they could from their home, but even that was too much. Told to abandon even their basic possessions at the water's edge, they crammed into the already overcrowded landing craft, like barrels of cheap wine and soured cabbage. Maybe his relatives in Grand Pré were aboard already. Maybe they were still somewhere in the chaos on shore. Maybe they'd escaped. He couldn't know. He also couldn't know the whereabouts of his father or his brother Jacques. The small landing craft groaned and heaved as it found its place on the outflowing tide. From the gunnel, Bénoni watched the water tumble over thick clumps of dark green seaweed, as his former life disappeared into the distance.

Grand Pré's wheat hardened yellow under curls of black smoke that cut lines like coal seams across the sky. Charred timber frames hung like the skeletons of giants. Heaps of ankle-length skirts, stockings, shoes carved from willow trees, black breeches, collarless wool shirts, and moccasins of moose and caribou rotted on the shoreline. Wooden trunks and bags of salted fish sat on the pale sand. The tide pushed ever upward as every day before. Hours later it pulled away, leaving a land dead and empty.

CHAPTER TWO

Jacques

Between them, Captain Murray and Colonel Winslow had crammed over 2,600 villagers into the holds of the transports and sent them to sea. Neither mentioned the final departure in writing, but they must have been relieved to see the Acadians off at long last. Colonel Robert Monckton had already drained the Isthmus of Chignecto and the surrounding communities of their Acadian populations.

The plan was to ply south, out of the Bay of Fundy, and into the Atlantic. They would meet up with Monckton's transports and form a convoy that would call at Annapolis Royal, where three more transports filled by John Handfield—commander of the former French capital once called Port-Royal—should have been waiting. Unlike the other commanders, Handfield hadn't sprung his trap quite so ruthlessly. Those he had to deport were his friends and his family. His wife was Acadian, as were most of his kin. When ships first pulled into the Annapolis Basin that August, most of the men fled into the woods. Charles Lawrence ordered Handfield to use "the most vigorous measures possible" to imprison the heads of households. Handfield disobeyed; he did not burn their houses or "destroy everything." He allowed the Acadians to gather themselves and prepare to leave. Those kindnesses put Handfield well behind schedule, so that when the convoy passed the Annapolis Basin in late October, Handfield's ships were not ready. They would have to sail later in the winter, when the weather was likely to be worse.

By now loaded aboard a ship, Jacques heard a gale picking up outside. The basin had sat calm and sickly green when he was last above deck, before the crew pulled anchor. Now the hull moaned with wind-slap and wave spray, a contralto voice filling out a chorus of anguish, fear, and the unmistakable sounds of seasickness. Few in the hold had spent any time at sea. None had ever been locked below deck like livestock. The stale air hung low along the floorboards, heavy with the stench of vomit and wet wool. Sheets of hail played a gloomy pizzicato on the iron-bolted hatches above the prisoners' heads. Some lay on their backs or sides. Most sat half upright against the damp posts and boards, their shoulders hunched, backs curled by sharp pains boiling up from their guts. The thin bands of orange light that cut through uneven cracks in the hull faded into the pale blue ink of night at sea.

The wind grew stronger. Jacques's wife, Catherine, was with him, as was his father, François, and his mother, Jeanne. They were spared the fate of many at the docks: they had boarded together. The loading was a frenzy. Children looked back from the landing crafts while their parents stood in the mass on land, still waiting their turn. Husbands scrambled to find their wives, sisters clung to one another, hoping they'd be put aboard together. No one knew where the ships were headed. Some families who were separated at the docks would never see each other again, and the confusion afforded no chance to say goodbye.

Waves shook the bow and flattened against the port side. Jacques knew the area well; these waves must mean the ship had rounded the cape and was headed for open water. Some prayed with craned necks; others lay wretched on their bedrolls and listened to the hail striking the deck above.

The North Atlantic behaves as though it has a temper like no other body of water on Earth. Black shoulders of swell heave. Whip-cracking gusts hurl the water through the air like shards of broken glass. Under the right conditions, wind and waves entangle and grow into massive storm systems that eat ships alive, and—if they make landfall—knock down forests and rip apart buildings. The most dangerous of these oceanic storms are tropical cyclones, commonly known as hurricanes.

These storms begin as a twist of hot sandy air whisking across the vast expanse of the Sahara Desert. Prevailing winds blowing from the east push the dry air toward the coast, where it mixes with cool, wet air curling up from tropical West Africa and the Gulf of Guinea, near Cape Verde. The mixed air draws moisture from the sea and rises high into the sky. Tiny water molecules crystalize and condense. In a flash, the microscopic shards shatter and hang in the air as if on strings: clouds. Cloud formation produces heat. As the air condenses, energy pushes outward. Air pressure drops. Slight high-level winds, common in late summer and early autumn, whisk this less dense air forward and dump it directly in the path of the growing system. As more air is pulled upward into the clouds, a vast region of low pressure develops. Air always moves toward areas of lower pressure. As the air rushes to the newly created void, it picks up speed: wind. As the pressure difference draws this wind back into the centre, the storm slows, starts to spin, and a cyclone is created.

In the middle of the ocean these storms are relatively harmless. Throughout winter, spring, and summer, they usually blow themselves out, disbanding into distinct thunderheads and rainstorms. In September and October, however, the African Easterly Jet arrives, its strong stream of wind three kilometres above the earth's surface. In January, it blows just five degrees north of the equator. By August, it has climbed into the thirteenth parallel and picked up speed. Gusting at an average of fifty kilometres per hour, the jet swallows up the storms that grow off Cape Verde and flings them deep into the tropical Atlantic. Once over warm ocean waters, these smaller storms strengthen and grow into gigantic systems of swirling clouds and fierce winds. Unlucky crews suffer these mid-ocean storms as nasty squalls. Near land, they grow into the largest storms on Earth.

If water temperatures stay above 26°C, these cyclones can strengthen into weather systems nearly eight hundred kilometres wide with sustained wind speeds over three hundred kilometres per hour. These autumnal systems usually slam first into the outer islands of the Caribbean, but slight changes in current direction or water temperature can push them up the coast to Florida or into the Gulf of Mexico. Sometimes, they head north.

This is what lay in store for Jacques LeBlanc, who knew nothing of oceanic storms, walls of black water, or winds that could suck the air out of your lungs. As he lay in the dark hold, his ears served as his only reference to what was growing outside. As storms approach ships at sea, those aboard often experience an unusually beautiful calm right before the first bands of wind hit. But the Acadian prisoners, trapped below, had no idea what they were about to sail into.

Five weeks before Jacques was crammed aboard the ship, while he and his father were still imprisoned at Fort Edward, one of the worst hurricanes in history grazed Pisiguit, signalling that this year on the North Atlantic would be especially harsh. It made landfall first in Virginia, far to the south of the colony of Nova Scotia. The *Virginia Gazette* reported on the damage days after it passed. "Most of the mill-dams are broke, the corn is almost laid level with the ground; many ships and other vessels drove ashore and damaged." Those in Les Mines experienced the storm as a heavy rain. Neither Murray nor Winslow felt compelled to record any observations about the weather. But St. John's, Newfoundland, "received a very severe stroke from the violence of a storm of wind," Robert Duff, the commodore governor, wrote. "A considerable number of boats, with their crews, have been totally lost." Nearly four thousand perished, mainly English and Irish sailors. The hurricane created a storm surge that raised the level of the harbour twenty feet above its normal height. Ships were tossed onto the hard rocks that flanked the harbour on all sides. It was the worst hurricane to ever hit the island and one of the deadliest Atlantic hurricanes on record.

In its wake, another storm was growing, and the Acadians were headed straight into its path. As Jacques and the rest of the prisoners rounded Cap Baptiste (known then to the English as Cape Porcupine, and now as Cape Blomidon), they felt the waves pounding the ship's sides.

The British did not record what occurred next. What happened to the fleet on the journey was of little concern to those safely on land. Once the ships left the Minas Basin, the prisoners became the responsibility of the New England governors who would receive them. But many years later, one nameless survivor of the trip would recount the fateful day of departure to Andrew Brown, a Presbyterian pastor living in Halifax. Brown's incomplete history of Nova Scotia—written some time during his stay in the colony between 1787 and 1795 and purportedly compiled in part from Acadian oral tradition—describes a poetic fall day of rusty skies and strong gales as the ships left the basin. "The reflections from the sky suddenly gave place to others from the land, that flitted as fast and which changed as they flitted from the bloody red to the sickly orange & the funeral black of the pine forest." Other survivors would mention the horrible trip in petitions to governors and town councils, written from the squalor of their new homes: conditions were crammed, food was scarce, the air was suffocating and stale, and fear gripped the prisoners.

Jacques and the convoy met a strong storm somewhere between the entrance to the Bay of Fundy, near where the town of Digby, Nova Scotia, sits today, and the entrance to Boston Harbour. The gale the transport ships met on their first night at sea, as recorded by Reverend Andrew Brown, was most likely an outer band of the storm. "During the night, this breeze freshened into a strong gale," he wrote, "& on reaching Cape Porcupine the waves rolled into mountains." When the ships finally made it to Boston ten days later, one captain reported it was the worst storm he had ever faced at sea. What he didn't know then was that he had also survived one of the largest earthquakes ever recorded.

Three days after the transport ships pulled anchor, just before ten in the morning, approximately 125 miles off the southernmost tip of Portugal, the sea floor cracked and rose. A vast column of water surged up and outward in wide concentric bands. The seismic energy rattled the Portuguese mainland, southern Spain, and the Atlantic coast of Morocco. Lisbon collapsed in a dusty gasp. Tens of thousands of people across two continents died under falling rubble, fire, and a massive storm surge. At sea, the ripple grew into a wall of water.

It hit Ireland less than two hours later. Kinsale's harbour filled and water flooded into the marketplace. Part of Galway's Spanish Arch, a section of the old city's wall, fell into the sea. Scotland's Loch Lomond suddenly rose about three feet above its banks before dropping to normal levels. Racing westward, the wave hit North America by mid-afternoon. The *Nancy*, a mid-size frigate, was somewhere off the island of St. Lucia when it felt the wave. The hull shuddered and groaned as if it had come aground hard. The crew, shaken and confused, threw a sounding line, only to find they were many leagues above the sea floor.

Nearby, off the island of St. Vincent, a crew reported themselves suspended sideways in the air for a few seconds, several feet above the deck. Their anchors, lashed and stowed, bounced heavily as the water dropped suddenly under the hull. The ship plummeted hard into the waves below, nearly sinking. The crew reported their sounding line turned yellow and smelled of sulphur shortly after. The tsunami entered the waters southwest of Nova Scotia as the fleet carrying Jacques and Bénoni plied the open blue Atlantic under stiff winds.

Rain, suspended in bands by seafoam-heavy air too thick to breathe, raked across the ceiling. Jacques heard the mast mount creak and twist under strain, producing eerie high-pitched noises like a thousand mice squeaking. Wave spray pummelled the hull-boards. The gale that had met the ships the evening they left had not blown itself out. Jacques didn't know how much time had passed, but steadily the weather outside the prison walls grew worse. The ship climbed the waves, seemed to hang in mid-air for just a second, and then crashed heavily into the flat water below. Everything went silent, like the ship was holding its breath. Jacques held his, too.

Sailors caught in storms like this often report strange and impossible-sounding events. One captain caught in a storm off the Caribbean on the same day as the Portuguese earthquake reported that the sky turned to copper and the ocean seemed to drop many feet out of nowhere. His ship spun in a wild direction, and before his cabin window three shards of green rock appeared in the sea, only to disappear minutes later when he fought his way to the deck. The ship survived. When conditions get like this, captains have three options: run, hold, or fight. Running pits both the ship and the savvy of its crew against nature's strongest weapon. Sailors need to carefully manage their sails to catch enough wind to outrun the storm without grabbing the full attention of the gust and capsizing. But masts can snap like matchsticks, sails can shred like tissue paper, and rigging can whip through the air like steel wire. Losing a mast, or two or three, in hurricane conditions is a death sentence.

Another option is to heave to: to halt forward movement by balancing rudder direction and sail catch. Steering hard into the wind while letting a small sail—usually a storm jib or a close substitute—catch toward the leeside can hold a ship almost in stasis, even in strong weather. Then the crew can try to wait out the storm below deck. In a hurricane, this is a risky operation.

If running and holding aren't options, sailors must fight. In hurricane-force winds, sails—designed to catch as much wind as possible — turn against their ships.

The sloops carrying the Acadian prisoners likely furled their mainsails and confronted the storm with an empty spar. The ships heaved and lurched through valleys of water with little control over their direction. To take a wave broadside is catastrophic, but rudders do not work without forward motion. With tight management of wind catch—utilizing a forward jib or storm sail—keen directional steering, and luck, ships can stay facing the waves and keep above water.

When the convoy hit the open water south of the colony of Nova Scotia, they engaged in a battle that may have lasted days. Over and over again the ships climbed walls of water while their occupants—prisoners and crew alike—feared that the next ridge would be too high and send them over backwards, plunging them beneath the waves. This is called pitch-poling, and if a crew can avoid it, floundering by pounding cross-waves, or suffering a fatal leak, they may survive the squall.

Some of the most harrowing stories of survival at sea come from the Irish diaspora. A century later but in very similar conditions to Jacques and the rest of the Acadian prisoners, Irish emigrants traversed the Atlantic from Ireland to North America, fleeing the great famine of the 1840s and 1850s. Many had no choice but to take passage on ramshackle "coffin ships"—sloops and schooners and brigs so heavily over-insured they were worth more to their owners if they sank than if they made it to the New World. Well over capacity, the coffin ships set out into the murderous seas of the North Atlantic regardless of weather. Many sank, losing all hands. Others barely survived mid-sea encounters with massive storms. Letters home and journals reveal stories of survival that best depict the experience of a storm at sea as a passenger on a wooden sailing ship.

Thomas Reilly, a young man from Dublin, was one of the lucky ones—barely. He left Dublin on February 19, 1848, and hoped for a swift passage to America. He transferred ships in Liverpool and, after a delay, finally hit the open ocean on March 1. He endured a series of storms throughout the journey before he eventually arrived, forlorn and weary, in New York, with a warning for future émigrés. In a letter home to his friend John M. Kelly, Reilly vividly recounts his crossing.

> Well I set sail and our ship, the *Patrick Henry*,
> was resolved to bring us to the South Sea Islands
> instead of to New York. We had the first two days
> very fair and rounded the Irish coast like a sea
> gull, the wind followed in our wake for three days
> on the Atlantic.
>   The forth day the Monsters of the deep
> showed their heads, the Captain said we would
> have a storm, and truly Boreas spent his rage on
> us that night. We were tumbled out of our berths,
> the hold was two feet full of water, a leak was
> gaining an inch a minute on us, our topsails were
> carried away, the most of male passengers were all
> night relieving each other at the pump and in the
> morning I left my hammock at seven o'clock to
> look at the terrible sea....
>   At five o'clock p.m. all hands were turned up
> to close reef sail, not a stitch of canvass to be seen

spread, six o'clock wind right ahead, the vessel lying to a rolling from side to side like a heavy log as she was, the passengers quaking with fear.

Ten o'clock, the scene below no light, the hatches nailed down, some praying, some crying some cursing and singing, the wife jawing the husband for bringing her into such danger, everything topsy turvy—barrels, boxes, cans, berths, children rolling about with the swaying vessel, now and again might be heard the groan of a dying creature, and continually the deep moaning of the tempest.

The scene above, bare poles, thunder and lightning, the ship almost capsized, lying on her beam, sheets of water drenching her decks, the sea swelling far above her masts, engulfing her around, and huge billows striking her bows and sides with the force and noise of a thousand sledge hammers upon so many anvils.

The ship receding with every wave, sometimes standing perpendicularly on her stern and shaking like a palsied man and then plunging decks and masts under water and raising to renew the same process. She would screech with every stroke of the waves, every bolt in her quaked, every timber writhed, the smallest nail had a cry of its own.

One o'clock in the morning, not a soul on the deck, standing upright, oh mercy one of our masts has gone over the side, bulwarks stoved in,

30 tons of water washing the decks from stern to
stern. The Captain is panic struck. Tom Reilly is
waiting on the quarter deck to get into her life
boat.

The captain speaks, carpenters cut away the
broken spars, look out for the next spar, here it
comes, The Mizen top is carried away. The ship
lurched on her side and lay in a state of distress
until day light.

Reilly, at least, was allowed above deck; he was not a prisoner
locked in a dank hold. He could see what was coming, even if he
was powerless to control what happened next.

If passenger manifests were taken for the ships, they haven't
survived. Jacques and Catherine, their children, and their
parents, were most likely aboard the *Seaflower*. The small sloop
registered at eighty-one tonnes, but it could handle storms and
was only eighteen passengers over its limit. Originally sent to
load prisoners from Grand Pré, the *Seaflower* was instead filled
with overflow passengers who had boarded in Pisiguit. If they
were among those transferred from the four vessels that loaded
below Fort Edward in late October—the *Neptune, Three Friends,
Dolphin,* and the *Ranger*—they were among the lucky ones.

At ninety tonnes, the *Ranger* was one of the larger sloops in
the fleet. In haste, Murray put 263 prisoners below deck, eighty-
one above capacity. Conditions must have been particularly
cramped and uncomfortable as prisoners sat face to face, even
lying on one another. At least they made it to their destination.
Not all of the ships did. The *Union*, packed with 392 prisoners at
Chignecto in October, departed for Pennsylvania. It was never

seen or heard from again. The sloop *Boscawen*, also loaded at Chignecto with 190 exiles and also expected to land at Pennsylvania, never arrived. Both ships presumably sank, killing everyone aboard.

The same storm that had hit Jacques's ship blew off course two larger ships: the brigantine *Experiment* and the snow *Edward*. They made landfall on the island of Antigua in the Caribbean some six weeks after leaving Nova Scotia, according to a March 1, 1756, report in the *New York Mercury*. Both ships resupplied and then set sail for their original destinations, eventually reaching Connecticut and New York, respectively, in mid-May. But of the 260 originally put aboard the *Edward*, approximately 150 survived the journey. The rest are reported to have died in an on-board outbreak of malaria.

Crammed together in such close quarters, the prisoners were particularly susceptible to ship-bound disease epidemics. Dysentery, malaria, and other common infections and viruses were prevalent. But one malady was more feared than any other, and it was perfectly at home in the holds' cramped and sordid conditions: smallpox.

The sores first showed inside the mouth and on the tongue. With the small red dots came fever and lethargy. The rash spread next to the face and neck, gradually consuming the entire body. The boils billowed and filled with opaque pus and hardened as they aged. Scabs formed and the skin began to flake. High fever and powerful aches racked the body. Death followed for some; survivors were left pebbled with pockmarks. Smallpox wasn't common in Acadia, so most of the prisoners had no immunity to the virus. Perhaps the soldiers who came from New England for the deportation brought the virus with them. Thirty years earlier, the disease had swept across Boston, infecting nearly six thousand (almost half the population of the fledgling city) and killing nearly nine hundred.

Viruses cannot reproduce on their own. Virions — tiny particles of virus without a host cell, a tenth of the size of a single cell of bacteria — are not organisms. They are strands of nucleic acid in a protective protein shell. Drifting through air and water, these particles seek out host cells. Once inside a living organism, they attack healthy cells and replicate themselves using the cell's own reproductive system. The new, identical viral particles are released from the original host cell, and further infect the body. One host infects another, and soon an outbreak occurs. In the musty air of a ship's hold, air worsened by the unseasonably warm weather the storm system had brought up from the Caribbean, the virus spread easily. An unguarded sneeze or a muffled cough would send virions into the air. With little circulation, nearby mouths would swallow the particles and regurgitate them back into the space. Cough. Sneeze. Spread.

Smallpox ripped through the lower decks of the transport convoy. Those already weak from months of imprisonment, rotten food, and bad water died quickly. The crew piled up the bodies on the decks. The *Ranger* lost 58; the *Endeavour* lost 51. The *Cornwallis*, filled with villagers from Chignecto, fared the worst, losing 210. By the time the ships made it to their destinations, over 1,000 prisoners in total would be dead, killed by disease, weather, or distress.

The storm that had battered the convoy gradually abated. The wind finally dropped. Slowly the shuddering in the hulls ceased. Jacques was relieved. The dead lay tangled among the living, but all his family members had survived. Some of the ships seized the opportunity to change course and pointed their bows toward Boston. The *Seaflower* was not among them. Perhaps blown off course by the weather, or delayed for repairs or another extenuating circumstance, the *Seaflower* did not arrive in Boston until November 15, nearly three weeks after the ship pulled anchor in the Minas Basin.

The portion of the fleet that headed for Boston after the storm passed did so only for repairs and supplies. The prisoners below their decks, including Bénoni and his family, were destined for colonies further south. If their ships were still in the harbour when the *Seaflower* finally arrived, it would have been the last time most of the family would be in the same place at the same time.

Anchored in the broad calm of Boston Harbour, Jacques did not feel relief. Although they had survived the storm, perhaps he sensed that what awaited them was merely a new form of horror.

CHAPTER THREE

Madeleine

The gangplank dropped with a heavy thud on the timbers of Boston's main pier. Madeleine, her husband, Amand Breau, and their five young children, Anne-Marie, Jean Baptiste, Joseph, Madeleine, and Marguerite, stood in the narrow opening left by the lowered walkway. Madeleine was only thirty-three years old, her husband just a year older. Anne-Marie, their oldest child, was only ten. Marguerite, still swaddled in rough-hewn hemp, had just seen her first birthday. The young family cowered amidst the noise of the busy pier. Shouting sailors and fellow prisoners swarmed past them in a blur. They'd been below deck long enough that any sight would have caught the eye, but this vantage of Boston was particularly striking. Twelve steep-pitched towers shot high above a tight wall of warehouse fronts, sail lofts, and merchant shops lining the water's edge. At the top of each steeple was a cross, all glowing in the morning sun. A fog of grey smoke clouded the streets that cut between the waterfront shops, concealing the innards of the city from Madeleine's exhausted eyes.

She stepped tentatively forward and was swept up by the mob. The stronger and more impatient attempted to run. Most hobbled, still feeling the effects of seasickness, hunger, and dehydration. From the bowels of the ship poured a terrible ooze of human suffering. To any Bostonians watching, the sight of the horde as they struggled ashore must have been nightmarish, like a scene from their coveted scripture, a ship sent up from hell to cleanse the city of its sins. But this wasn't their first encounter with the destitute exiles.

Roughly two weeks before Madeleine and her family arrived in Boston, six ships — the *Dolphin, Endeavour, Neptune, Ranger, Sarah and Molly,* and *Three Friends* — had limped into the harbour, seeking repair and shelter. The transports had cut into the harbour on the morning of November 5, fleeing an awful storm. They had been at sea only a week but were battered badly. They had left the Minas Basin as part of the larger convoy of prisoner transports, but the group had been scattered early on by the tempestuous weather. The half-dozen that sailed into Boston on the fifth were not scheduled to land any prisoners; they were destined for ports farther south. When the Massachusetts assembly heard of their arrival, they sent a group of investigators to assess the condition of the ships. The investigators didn't like what they found.

On the *Dolphin* they found the prisoners "sickly, occasioned by being too much crowded, 40 lying on deck, and their water very bad." The ships' provisions were already seriously depleted, and the exiles were in poor physical condition from the prolonged imprisonment below deck and the rough voyage. The assemblymen ordered the prisoners removed from the overcrowded ships. The ships' intended capacity of two persons per ton would be adhered to, new water would be put aboard, and the fleet would return to sea as soon as possible. The news infuriated the captains. According to the terms they'd agreed to with Lieutenant-Governor Lawrence, their pay depended on the successful delivery of all prisoners to their prescribed destinations. To assuage the captains, the assembly brought in Benjamin Green, a member of the governor's council of Nova Scotia. He assured the captains they would still be paid their full rate, even if they left some of their cargo in Boston.

Maybe they chose most sick prisoners to disembark at Boston. Or the elderly and young. Perhaps they simply reached into the dark hold and grabbed limbs at random. Whoever they were, those gathered on the decks of the battered fleet squinted, trying to focus their weary eyes on their new home as they prepared to go ashore. They were the first of hundreds of exiles who would land in the city over the coming weeks. The prisoners left below deck probably wondered what fate would befall those taken ashore. Reprovisioned, repaired, and with a little more room in the holds, the ships pulled anchor and tacked south on a cold November breeze, aiming for Maryland and Virginia.

Madeleine had never seen a city before, and the commotion of the busy Boston waterfront shocked her already frayed nerves. Sailors and stevedores shouted sharp, unfamiliar words. Behind her sat Long Wharf, a nearly 875-yard-long wooden hulk extending far into the harbour. Madeleine stood at the foot of the wharf and marvelled at the cityscape. The broad entrance of King Street, the city's most important artery, began where the pier met the land. Lined with shops, stores, and taverns, King Street was where Bostonians of all classes mingled in search of food, drink, slaves, and companionship. Years later, John Hancock, Paul Revere, Samuel Adams, and other Boston members of the Sons of Liberty would gather here, convening secret meetings and laying the foundations for the American Revolution.

The weary Acadian prisoners were likely relieved to at least find their feet on solid ground. Their keepers ordered them to form a line. Madeleine cast her eyes around to make sure her family was together, and then lowered her head for the march forward. The prisoners were led west through the narrow streets, away from the harbour, to a makeshift camp on the Boston Common until the assembly could agree on a more permanent solution. The common was windswept and yellow, its grass trampled low by grazing herds of cows and goats. At the centre of the common stood a massive elm tree. (When it was measured in 1825, it had a base circumference of over seventeen feet.)

Boston was governed in the strict code of the reformed settlers who first landed there a century earlier. Believing the Church of England to be inadequately reformed, splinter cells of nonconformists began organizing around their common desire to purify the church of its Catholic practices. Facing persecution in England, thousands of Puritan dissenters had fled to the New World in the early seventeenth century in the hope they could establish a home where they could freely practise their beliefs. Their vision had become a reality to a degree that they themselves had not likely imagined. Where other early settlements in New England failed, Boston thrived. Cotton Mather, the prominent Puritan reverend, credited this success to the city's founding ethics, as he observes in his book (one of nearly 450 he wrote) *Magnalia Christi Americana*:

There were more than a few attempts of the
English to people and improve the parts of
New England which were to the northward of
New Plimouth. But the designs of those attempts
being aimed no higher than the advancement
of some worldly interest, a constant series of
disasters has confounded them, until there was
a plantation erected upon the nobler designs of
Christianity; and that plantation, though it has
had more adversaries than perhaps any one upon
earth, yet, having obtained help from God, it
continues to this day."

Mather wasn't the only one of this opinion. The theocrats
who ruled Boston in the early days of the colony saw their city
as a holy place and fought hard for their version of purity. Those
who didn't believe in the Puritan interpretation of Christianity
were subject to slander, beatings, and even death. Among
accused witches and criminals, four Quakers were hanged from
the great elm tree on Boston Common for refusing to repent
their beliefs.

By the time the Acadians arrived late in 1755, Boston had
become slightly more tolerant, but not by much. Catholics were
still viewed with hostility as idolatrous papists. Some Bostonians
feared the new arrivals might steal their ships and flee under
the cover of darkness. The *Boston Gazette* published a letter from
one citizen concerned that the Acadians would even destroy the
city itself by lighting fire to the powder house while "heated with
Passion and Popish Zeal."

Despite the hostile atmosphere, Madeleine and her family attempted to settle into their "temporary shelter," most likely a tent. More exiles arrived daily at the Boston Common camp. Familiar faces appeared in the flat winter light. Nearly all the prisoners unloaded at Boston that season hailed from the Les Mines area. Across the sprawl of barracks and tents, fires of green early-season wood smouldered, choking up thick smoke. Forlorn exiles wandered from structure to structure, calling out for missing loved ones. Distant cousins, in-laws, and friends waved and pointed, urging Madeleine farther along the ranks, telling her that her parents, François and Jeanne, and her brother Jacques and his family were somewhere on the bleak yellow field in the heart of colonial Boston. If nothing else, she had her family. But their happiness and relief at seeing one another was likely short-lived. After less than two weeks in the city, word spread through the camp that they were moving again. Madeleine prayed that this time everyone in her family would travel together. The members of the Assembly of Massachusetts, like Charles Lawrence, feared that, in the event of war, the nearly one thousand Acadians would side with the French, people with whom they shared a language and a religion. And as 1755 drew to a close, war seemed imminent.

The Ohio Country was a relatively small area, cross-hatched with rivers and stands of centuries-old hardwood forests. Here the Monongahela and Allegheny Rivers joined to form the Ohio River, the largest tributary of the Mississippi.

The land was home to many Indigenous groups, including the Shawnee, Haudenosaunee (Iroquois), Lenape (Delaware),

(Illinois), Myaamia (Miami), Wyandot (Huron), Odawaa (Ottawa), Anishinaabe (Chippewa), Kiikaapoa (Kickapoo), Potawatomi, Kaskaskia, Mingo, and the Erie. In the seventeenth century, explorer René-Robert Cavelier had laid claim to exclusive trading rights in both the Ohio Valley and the Great Lakes region.

As the British expanded westward from the Atlantic coast they also began trading with the Indigenous Peoples. They came for fur pelts, particularly beaver. Before the Europeans' exploration of North America, hat-makers and tailors relied mainly on furs from Russia, harvested from wolves, foxes, martens, and stoats. Waterproof beaver hats became immensely popular across the continent, offering both protection from the rain and a sign of social status. The Indigenous Peoples trapped the beavers and harvested the furs, which they sewed into garments. Daily use rubbed the coarse longer hairs off the coats, leaving behind the soft under-fur. Such garments were now ready for trading. They traded the pelts for iron tools, weapons, and alcohol, among other items. European traders shipped the pelts back to France and England for processing. The fur trade drove the European exploration and colonization of the New World.

Traders poured into the region throughout the late seventeenth and early eighteenth centuries, disrupting local alliances, trading networks, and friendships. Conflict was inevitable as both sides, the British and the French, sought to control the lucrative territory. Each fortified their trading posts, and soldiers flooded into the region. Cursory attempts at diplomacy quickly descended into skirmishes and violence. Casualties began to pile up. The Indigenous Peoples were forced to choose sides in the fight over their own land. To the English and French, control over the Ohio River lands meant not only control over the economic future of the New World but also continental dominance.

In July 1755, Major General Edward Braddock led a British expedition against Fort Duquesne, on the site of what is now the city of Pittsburgh. Braddock's forces were within six miles of the French fort when the roar of muskets echoed through the forest. Burnt powder tinged the air rain-cloud grey. Surrounded by a small but deadly coalition of French marines and Indigenous warriors, the redcoats fired wildly into the forest. From the deep woods and rocky outcrops on both sides of the rough road came endless volleys of iron musket balls. Amidst the ambush a single bullet sliced through Braddock's ribcage, into the soft membrane of his lungs, and he dropped from his horse. After three hours, the surviving British fled, leaving the bodies of the decimated regiment scattered like fallen leaves on the forest floor. Fewer than half of the 1,300 escaped, unscathed physically but scarred by memories of the ungodly racket released upon them in that forested corridor.

British commanders, keen to retaliate for Braddock's humiliating defeat, were planning another attack. Few in Massachusetts were happy to see a group of French-speaking exiles arrive, as tensions flared just a few hundred miles to the west. But as good Puritans, they could not refuse to accept the enfeebled prisoners, either. The plan was to house the Acadians temporarily and then divide them into smaller groups and send them to the towns that dotted the colony's rural landscape. Isolated among people who did not speak their language or share their religion, they would have to assimilate to survive.

Assimilation is a common strategy employed in ethnic-cleansing schemes. Forced assimilation strips people of their cultural foundations. The dominant culture seeks to fill the void so gradually that it can seem inevitable, even natural. A recent example of this strategy is the residential school system that existed in Canada from the 1880s to 1996. Through this program, the Canadian government removed, often with force, an estimated 150,000 Indigenous children from their homes and placed them in residential schools. In theory, the schools were intended to meet the provisions of the 1876 Indian Act, which required the government to provide an education for Indigenous youth and prepare them to live a self-sufficient Euro-Canadian life. In reality they were part of a systemic push to destroy Indigenous culture and sovereignty. Survivors of the residential school system report experiencing physical, sexual, and psychological abuse. Tuberculosis and influenza flourished in the overcrowded, unhygienic environments. Today, the schools' devastating legacy continues to emanate in troubling rates of addiction, incarceration, poverty, and domestic violence among Indigenous populations. As many subjected to the residential school system would discover, the first step of assimilation was usually isolation. Isolation from friends, family, and one's culture as a whole.

Madeleine and her family, including her parents and her brother Jacques, were sent to Braintree, a small town a little over twelve miles south of Boston. They likely walked the distance, arms wrapped around the few possessions they still had from home. It was an unusually warm winter, but sharp winds off the North Atlantic would have stung their exposed skin and numbed their fingers.

The citizens of Braintree looked with contempt from their homes the day the Acadian prisoners arrived in town. Young men were leaving Massachusetts's small towns in droves to prepare to fight. As parents said goodbye to their sons headed for battle, it is not hard to imagine they would carry some prejudice toward the group of foreign exiles now appearing in their communities.

Madeleine was settled in a small home with her husband and five children. Her parents were housed nearby with Jacques, Catherine, and their three children. At first, the authorities more or less left the exiles to fend for themselves. Some, like Madeleine and her family, stayed where they were put, dedicating most of their time to surviving the winter on alms and donated goods. The more physically fit or determined weren't so stationary. During the first winter, some Acadians attempted to find their way home. By land and sea they forged into a northeastern winter in search of their old farms and livelihoods. Some took jobs on merchant ships heading north, others simply packed up and headed home on foot. Some roamed the colony, searching for family members and friends spread throughout small towns similar to Braintree. The LeBlanc clan might have entertained similar plans, but François and Jeanne were elderly, and Madeleine's youngest child was not yet two.

Freedom of movement around the colony didn't last long for the exiles. In April 1756, the assembly passed a law prohibiting captains from hiring Acadians to crew sailing ships. One month later, another law passed forbidding Acadians to leave the limits of their assigned towns under penalty of flogging. Flogging whips were made from thick pieces of cotton rope braided together from three smaller ropes — themselves braided from three strands of cotton — and unravelled at the end into nine strips of knotted cotton cord. Swung hard against a bare-skinned back, the individual strips clawed parallel marks into the flesh, giving the whip its distinctive name, the cat-o'-nine-tails. Often performed in public, flogging tortured both the body and mind, at once maiming and humiliating. The standard punishment for lesser offences was twelve lashes, which was likely the punishment for Acadians caught outside their town limits. Once apprehended, the offenders were stripped of their shirts and strung by the hands from a post or overhead beam. The whip-holder drew the hard nine-tailed cord over his shoulder and paused.

Herman Melville, in his fictionalized memoir *White-Jacket*, gives a lurid description of a common naval flogging on the man-of-war he worked while serving as a young sailor in the American navy in the nineteenth century. Melville's account suggests what a wandering Acadian prisoner could have faced in the spring of 1756 if caught roaming the Massachusetts countryside.

> The Captain's finger was now lifted, and the first boatswain's-mate advanced, combing out the nine tails of his cat with his hand, and then, sweeping them round his neck, brought them with the whole force of his body upon the mark. Again, and again, and again; and at every blow, higher and higher rose the long, purple bars on the prisoner's back. But he only bowed over his head, and stood still. Meantime, some of the crew whispered among themselves in applause of their ship-mate's nerve;

but the greater part were breathlessly silent as the
keen scourge hissed through the wintry air, and
fell with a cutting, wiry sound upon the mark.

The Acadian exiles were stuck: their freedom to move
denied, their opportunities for employment restricted, and
their rights to land lost, rendering them unable to search for
missing family or improve their own situations. They were
incarcerated without chains or shackles, surrounded by people
who resented them not only because they spoke French and
practised a religion that the predominant Puritans abhorred,
but also because they were dependent upon the public purse.

In 1757, nearly two years after their arrival in Massachusetts,
an official census was taken of the Acadian population. At the
time, many of the exiles were not working. They had no land
nor the means to purchase any, and their general inability
to speak English combined with common prejudice against
them excluded most from the trades and crafts that typically
employed the rural poor. The voyage had apparently been
hardest on François; he was described as an "invalid, incapable
of labour." Jacques, Madeleine's brother, was noted as "weakly"
but "capable in part." Perhaps, like their father, he was unable to
recover from the journey or had suffered from illness or injury.
Madeleine, in contrast, was "incapable of labour" because she
was "obviously pregnant and about to give birth," which suggests
that she was relatively healthy. Amand, her husband, was listed
as healthy, but their oldest daughter, Anne-Marie, twelve at
the time, was categorized as weakly. Amand's parents and his
brother and his family were also in Braintree at the time of the
census. They were faring little better than the LeBlanc family,

with only two of the seven members listed as capable of labour and the rest weakly, invalid, or "subject to fits."

Perhaps the census-takers focused on the Acadians' fitness for work because the authorities wanted to take stock of the exiles' ability to rebel. By 1757, the war in Ohio Country between the English and the French had spilled into the mountain and lake country of northern New York and near the border with New France. That summer, French forces under the command of General Louis-Joseph de Montcalm, allied with a large militia of fighters from various regional Indigenous Nations, decimated the poorly armed British forts. As the French and Indigenous forces grew more powerful, and as the battles grew closer to Massachusetts' western border, fears in the colony of an Acadian-French conspiracy likely reignited.

It is also likely that the census-takers were driven by budgetary concerns. Towns like Braintree were responsible for supplying the exiles with housing and basic necessities until they could provide for themselves. The general court would reimburse the towns for these expenses, and the Nova Scotia colonial administration would reimburse the general court. The protracted process of reimbursement made some town councils wary of spending more than was absolutely necessary, and some towns were notably thriftier than others.

In Methuen, a small town near the modern-day border with New Hampshire, Laurence Mius, an exile from Cap Sable, was paid "three rods of old cloth, two pounds of dried cod and one pound of pork fat" for two months of work. When he complained to the local overseer of the poor, he was beaten with an iron poker, causing him to "spit blood for the rest of the day." His complaint of the incident fell on deaf ears. John Labrador from

Île Royale complained to the town council of Wilmington, a town not far from Methuen, that he and his seven children were settled in a house with neither doors nor a roof. In response to a petition he sent after a storm flooded his house, the council advised him to "build a boat."

In the summer of 1756, acting on orders from the assembly, the selectmen who comprised local government began plucking Acadian children from their homes and forcing them to work in English-speaking homes. Indentured service was common at the time; many of the British colonists had themselves served indentured work terms. A typical contract required the servant to commit to a number of years of work in exchange for passage. Ostensibly, the plan would prepare the Acadian children to support themselves. They would be removed from their destitute families to be taught trades and crafts, learn to speak English, and abandon Catholicism. More importantly and perniciously, providing the British colonists with cheap labour and reducing the number of Acadians dependent on the towns for support also accelerated the assimilation process.

Madeleine's oldest daughter, twelve-year-old Anne-Marie, was the perfect age to be taken away. Each time a Braintree official came near her home, Madeleine shuddered and reached for Anne-Marie, never sure if it was her time to go. Eighteen miles away, in the coastal town of Marshfield, Joseph Michel, an exile from Port-Royal, watched as the town's selectmen took his two sons. Relocated to Plymouth, they were separated and indentured to a farmer and a fisherman. The youngest, Paul, was just fifteen.

Joseph Michel did not sit resigned to his fate after his sons were taken. Neither did Jean Landry of Chelmsford, Claude

Benoit of Oxford, Claude and Pierre LeBlanc and Charles Daigle of Concord, Augustin LeBlanc of Worcester, Jacques Hebert and Joseph Vincent of Andover, or Antoine Hebert of Waltham, when their children were taken. They petitioned for their children's return by baring their sorrow. "The loss of our homes, being brought here, and separated one from another are as nothing to what we now experience: the forcible taking away of our children from before our very eyes. Nature can not endure this. Were the choice ours, we would rather give up body and soul than be separated from our children. Hence, we appeal to your mercy and your honor that you will have the good will to end this cruelty," they wrote. Other aggrieved parents submitted similar pleas. In a rare act of compromise, the general court agreed to remove Acadian children from their parents' homes only when absolutely necessary for their health or well-being.

Anne-Marie was safe, but Madeleine probably worried that a different sort of visitor would take another member of her family. Her father was seventy-six and ill. If he were to die in Braintree, he would not rest in peace. The Catholics had no churches, no priests, no burying grounds. In Grand Pré funerals were large community affairs, with hundreds of friends and family in attendance and a proper funeral Mass. Funerals in Massachusetts perplexed Madeleine. Large black-clad groups walked solemnly and silently by the house. A group of young men carried the dead in an austere pine coffin draped in a black pall. No one eulogized the deceased; no one spoke much at all.

Madeleine felt trapped. If they fled and were caught, they'd be flogged—or worse. And where would they go? War lay to the west. To the south was only deeper into British territory. The sea flanked them to the east, and the ports were under constant watch. Their only possible refuge was north, to New France, but Madeleine knew her parents could never survive the trip. Any thoughts of escape would have to wait.

Perhaps Madeleine counted herself lucky that she knew where her parents and her brother Jacques and his family were. She wondered if her brothers Bénoni and Jean Baptiste had survived the deportation and, if so, where they had landed. And what about her sisters Cécile and Anne? She had seen them in Grand Pré the day the ships were loaded, but where the winds had taken them after that was anyone's guess.

CHAPTER FOUR

Anne

Pesthouses—also known as lazarettos, fever sheds, and plague houses—became fixtures in European towns and cities in the Middle Ages to help prevent the spread of deadly diseases. The pesthouse in Philadelphia, built in 1743 on Province Island, near the confluence of the Schuylkill and Delaware Rivers, was the first of its kind in British North America. The purpose of Philadelphia's pesthouse was to quarantine those arriving at the city's port who were suffering from highly contagious diseases, such as smallpox, cholera, and typhus. The sick were forcibly contained in the pesthouse with little expectation of recovery. It was here that Pennsylvania's deputy governor, Robert Hunter Morris, grudgingly agreed to land the nearly four hundred Acadian exiles who appeared like an early snowfall on the calm waters of the Delaware River in mid-November 1755. Among them was Anne Landry, née LeBlanc.

She was the third of François and Jeanne LeBlanc's twelve children and their oldest daughter. Anne was forty-seven years old and the mother of ten when her husband, Germain, to whom she had been married for twenty-six years, joined the rest of the men of Grand Pré to hear Colonel John Winslow's message on that fateful September day. Germain's family was originally from Pisiguit, but he settled in the Grand Pré area in the small hamlet of Village des Melanson after marrying. Germain was likely a farmer, as most men in the community were. Occasionally he would have been called on to build and repair dikes, his duty as a member of the community. Anne would likely have spent her days tending the family gardens, cooking and washing, and rearing their children. By 1755, the oldest of their brood had married and started families of their own.

When the day of deportation came, Anne, Germain, and their dependent children were loaded on one of the smaller sloops, either the *Hannah* or the *Swan*, carrying 140 and 168 prisoners respectively. Both ships survived the storm that nearly destroyed the entire fleet. On November 20, they dropped anchor just southwest of Philadelphia. And there they sat, for four long, miserable days.

Philadelphia neither expected nor wanted hundreds of Acadian exiles to land on its shore any more than Boston had. As soon as the ships were sighted on the Delaware River, Deputy Governor Robert Morris was notified. Morris was of the opinion that the Acadians were not neutrals but "Traitors and Rebels to the crown of Great Britain," and he shared the popular fear that the exiles would ally themselves with other Catholics in Philadelphia and conspire against the British. He promptly called on the city assembly to decide what to do. While they argued, Morris ordered the captains to keep the prisoners aboard and then scribbled letters to prominent officials throughout British America to seek their advice.

Jonathan Belcher, the governor of New Jersey, replied swiftly to Morris's letter. He shared Morris's fearful and suspicious views and vowed that he would do "all in my power to crush an attempt" by the Acadians to land in his colony. Belcher was the father of the Chief Justice of the Supreme Court of Nova Scotia, who had strongly supported Charles Lawrence's expulsion order, declaring it necessary and entirely legal. But Morris's hands were tied by the assembly, many of whom were devout Quakers. Whether or not he was opposed to landing the Acadians in his colony, he had peers to appease, and diplomacy eventually won out. A sympathetic Huguenot turned prominent Quaker, Anthony Benezet went out to the sloops to speak with the exiles. He reported to the assembly that the prisoners were badly in need of "blankets, shirts, stockings, and other necessities." (Benezet apparently acted to provide the prisoners with some form of relief, for assembly records show that he was later reimbursed for expenses he incurred on behalf of the exiles.) The assembly urged Morris to land the exiles before winter. Morris agreed and, in light of an epidemic of smallpox sweeping through the ships' holds, stipulated that the prisoners be taken to the pesthouse on Province Island.

Philadelphia, the city of brotherly love (from the Greek root *philo* meaning love, and *adelphos* meaning brother or brethren), was founded on the Quaker principles of equality. Born in seventeenth-century England, Quakerism came to the New World with the arrival of William Penn, a staunch supporter of the sect and thus a theological enemy of the Crown. Using the connections of his father, a powerful admiral, Penn secured the largest charter of land given to any private citizen and sailed to North America to establish a Quaker colony where everyone would be equal and accepted. The colony's government would not be affiliated with any one faith, and citizens were to be granted complete religious freedom. Penn sought to make his colony a model for all to follow, and the founding ideals of Pennsylvania may have helped to inspire the Declaration of Independence and the first Bill of Rights. In keeping with his Quaker tenets, Penn also sought to deal fairly with the local Indigenous Peoples in matters of land acquisition and trade.

Putting these ideals into effect proved difficult. William Penn returned to England at the start of the eighteenth century and left the stewardship of the colony in the hands of his sons, Thomas and Richard. They were not as idealistic as their father, and Pennsylvania began to stray even further from its foundational Quaker principles. Although Catholicism was tolerated and the Jesuits were allowed to establish several churches, they remained a minority that the Protestants often looked down upon, or worse. Religious strife in the colony often flared into violence. In 1740, and again in 1755, angry mobs of Presbyterians descended on the only Catholic church in the city, St. Joseph's, intent on reducing it to rubble. Anglican leaders who found themselves embroiled in scandal were branded closeted papists and publicly derided. For instance, John Ury, an Anglican priest accused of masterminding an alleged plot by slaves to burn the city of New York to the ground in 1741, was described by Philadelphia newspapers as "the Romish Priest." Even George Whitefield, the popular travelling Anglican preacher and evangelist, was alleged to be "supported under hand by deists and Jesuits or both." Anti-Catholic propaganda drastically overstated the number of Catholics in Pennsylvania, advancing the belief that the colony was on the verge of a religious takeover. Concerned Philadelphia citizens petitioned the city, unsuccessfully, to shut down St. Joseph's, fearful that Catholic services would only allow the "popish virus" to spread through the community.

However, at least on paper and in the courts, Penn's tenets protected the Catholics of the colony. St. Joseph's stayed open. Citizens could worship however they wanted. But only Christians were allowed to hold office, and nearly all came from the Quaker elite. Relations with the Indigenous Peoples also failed to live up to Penn's ideals. The Pennsylvania government routinely stole their land by drafting complicated and highly unfair treaties.

By the time Anne arrived on the Delaware River in November 1755, Pennsylvania was embroiled in a territorial war with the Indigenous Peoples and the French on the western frontier. The colony was rife with the kind of francophobia and anti-Catholic sentiment that the deputy governor had expressed when first confronted with the question of the Acadian exiles. Anne must have felt relief when, after a harrowing sea voyage and four long days at anchor, the hatch bolts popped open and the morning sunlight pierced the ink-thick darkness of the hold. She would quickly discover, though, that Philadelphia was not a friendly place.

The dock at Province Island slowly arranged into sharper and sharper lines as Anne's eyes adjusted to the November sun. Before her sat several stout wooden buildings and a growing crowd of dishevelled exiles. The soldiers and sailors around them hustled the prisoners toward one particular building; they seemed anxious to get the exiles inside and then leave, their faces grim and tense, almost afraid.

Anne, Germain, and the rest of the nearly four hundred exiles likely bedded down on simple cots lined in rows inside the basic structure. Pesthouses were not hospitals; they were not built to heal the sick but rather to keep them segregated from the general population. The symbolism of being an unwanted people sent to such a place was probably not lost on Anne or any other Acadian sent to the pesthouse that winter. Whether or not they were actually sick was immaterial. In the eyes of the city council, *they* were the perceived disease, and their placement in the pesthouse was to prevent their contaminating the good people of the city. All Anne could do was try to stay alive while she hoped her situation would change.

The winds of early winter cut through the exterior walls and stirred the damp and dangerous air inside. It's easy to imagine Anne dreaming of her warm hearth in Grand Pré, where the smell of thick vegetable stew simmering in the early evening would have filled her home. The harvest would have been finished, the dikes solid with frozen earth. The short days and cold weather of December would have meant more time inside, mending clothing, preserving food, socializing with friends and family, and preparing for the winter that lay ahead. It would have been painful to recall those times as Anne and her family lay prone in rows, surrounded by feverish fits of coughing, sorrowful moans, and the foul odours of the sickroom.

Morris and the assembly members knew they shouldn't leave the exiles confined in the pesthouse all winter, but they were divided on exactly where the Acadians should be sent. Like their peers in Massachusetts, many officials wanted to disperse the group throughout the rural counties and let local overseers of the poor take charge of their welfare. However, more pressing than a permanent solution to the Acadian relocation was the assembly's winter adjournment. The assemblymen retired to their warm homes for the winter season and left their official duties behind, without a cogent plan. Anne and the rest were left to rot. In the cold and bleak atmosphere of the pesthouse, Germain fell ill. The records do not state exactly when he died, but by the beginning of 1756 he was gone. It was likely smallpox or a similar deadly virus. Many other exiles perished during the winter months. They were buried in Southeast Square, later renamed Washington Square, just one block from the State House.

Jean Baptiste Galerne had been a deputy in the village of Pisiguit before the Expulsion. In the winter of 1756, he composed an emotional appeal to the Philadelphia assembly. Galerne's petition described the Acadians' perspective of events that led up to the Expulsion and attempted to convey the extent of the exiles' suffering. Galerne was careful to extend gratitude to the citizens of Philadelphia, whom he thanked for their "Sympathy, Benevolence, and Christian charity," but he stressed the Acadians' losses. "We were made Prisoners," he told the assembly, "and our Estates, both real and personal, forfeited for the King's Use," and then "banished from our native Country, and reduced to live by Charity in a Strange land." Galerne concluded his petition with a simple request: that the king and Britain compensate the "poor distressed and afflicted People."

Morris convened a special session of the assembly to address Galerne's petition. Two weeks after Galerne's message was delivered to the State House, the assemblymen passed a motion to allow Anthony Benezet and other friends of the exiles to relocate them throughout the counties near Philadelphia, and they made money available for provisions and housing. Families would be kept together, but no more than one family would be sent to each township. Welfare would be provided for twelve months, and then the assembly would decide whether or not to extend it. Those able to farm would receive some farmland and animals. From these provisions, officials hoped that within the one-year period the exiles would be self-sufficient.

This plan was an improvement over quarantine in the pest-house, but it rested on two assumptions: that the Acadians would agree to be separated from one another and the towns would willingly accept the exiles. Both assumptions were wrong. The assemblymen may have wondered why the exiles would refuse the opportunity to resume their former way of life and support themselves. But the Acadians recognized that sending each family to a separate town would have meant social and cultural isolation. Instead of forcing the contested issue, the assembly ordered the Acadians moved from Providence Island to Philadelphia proper.

Anne had never seen such a large place. Over twelve thousand people called Philadelphia home by 1756. Because of its central location and Penn's founding principle of tolerance, the city had become the largest and most important in the colonies. Immigrants from Europe flocked to the riverside port, and the city flourished as a hub of modernity. By 1757 the city's streets were lit with glass lamps containing oil candles, the first street lights in North America. Philadelphia's first college graduated its first class the same year. Theatre troupes touring the colonies during the middle of the decade brought Shakespeare's *Othello* to the city's small theatre (one of only a handful in North America). And the *Pennsylvania Gazette*, one of the few newspapers in British North America at the time, could be found on many street corners.

Philadelphia's most famous citizen, the polymath Benjamin Franklin, first began making a name for himself as the publisher of the *Gazette* before going on to become a celebrated statesman, scientist, inventor, author, and diplomat. Franklin made important breakthroughs in the study of electricity and founded the city's hospital and its first college, which would grow into an Ivy League research centre. Inspired by the coffee houses of London, Franklin had established the Junto, a discussion group that evolved into the Library Company of Philadelphia, one of the most valuable collections of literary and historical manuscripts in North America, with over five hundred thousand books, including the first editions of Herman Melville's *Moby-Dick* and Walt Whitman's *Leaves of Grass*. In addition to his own inventions, he improved on the work of others, designing better street lamps, musical instruments, and stoves. The bustling city was nothing like the quiet Acadian villages the exiles like Anne knew and loved.

A 1763 sketch from the perspective of the eastern bank of the Delaware River shows Philadelphia spread wide and low, clinging to the western riverbank. Four large church steeples and clusters of three- and four-storey buildings with low-angled, pitched roofs mark the skyline. Small piers jut into the river, and beyond the city to the northwest lies a low range of hills.

The city's layout reflected traditional British colonial style: a grid of straight east-west and north-south streets with a larger commercial street through the middle of town, stretching from the docks to the outskirts, aptly named Market Street.

Anne and many other exiles were settled in the poorest city district, near Pine Street, between Fifth and Sixth Streets. They lived in small one-storey wooden houses, which the locals quickly dubbed "neutral huts." Luckily for the Acadians, their friend Anthony Benezet lived nearby, and the church of St. Joseph's, the only Catholic place of worship in the city, was only a few blocks away. Though they had little, they were relatively safe in this, their own miniature district within the vast city. Acadian names began to appear in the parish records of St. Joseph's. Marriages, births, and baptisms were noted, and the registers quickly filled with Landrys, Blanchards, Doirons, and LeBlancs.

But life in the city wasn't easy for Anne, by now a widow with at least four children to support. A job was out of the question. Far from the vast fields and bounty of Acadia, Anne likely had to beg for food for her children and straw to stuff in the walls of her tiny hut to stave off the cold. The provisional welfare was meant to afford them the bare necessities, but it seemed to fail. Another friend of the exiles, William Griffitts, noted as much in a plea to the assembly in October 1756. Griffitts reported that as many as fifty Acadians had already died from smallpox, and many more would have succumbed if not for the care of doctors and nurses who donated their time to help. He described the survivors as starving: "many of them have had neither meat nor bread for many weeks together, and been necessitated to pilfer and steal for the support of life."

The exiles submitted a series of petitions to the colonial assembly and to Thomas and Richard Penn, who were in England at the time, demanding to know whether they were being treated as British subjects or prisoners of war. It was an important distinction. Prisoners of war in the eighteenth century were guaranteed certain rights—at least the ones with white skin. Under the terms of the Treaty of Westphalia, signed at the end of the Thirty Years War, prisoners of war acquired the right to be exchanged for other prisoners of war. By the time of the Expulsion, both the British and French routinely traded prisoners, and official recognition as prisoners of war could mean the opportunity to go to one of the French colonies.

Alexis Thibaudeau, one of the exiles in Pennsylvania, explained to the assembly that Charles Lawrence had told the Acadians they were prisoners. He demanded "the same privileges which French prisoners enjoyed," including "leave to depart to our Nation; or any where, to join our country people." Oliver Tibaudat stated the exiles were eager to "join with our Nation in some Place," and wanted to know "whether we are Subjects, Prisoners, Slaves, or Freemen?" Tibaudat persisted in his own reply. Surely they were not subjects, he argued, because the king would never "oppress his Subjects in the Manner we have been oppressed." Nor could they be considered slaves, as "Christians have never made a trade of such as believe in Jesus Christ." The British had stolen their land, deported them, and denied them freedom of movement, so they couldn't be considered freemen. Therefore, Tibaudat concluded, they must be prisoners, "For we must be something, or be reduced to a state of non-existence."

The assembly responded to the demand for formal recognition with a plan to stamp out any discussion of the exiles' status in the colony. John Campbell, the 4th Earl of Loudoun, commander-in-chief in North America, and governor general of Virginia, was especially upset by the situation in Pennsylvania. He viewed the petitions as evidence that the Acadians were becoming politicized. This was dangerous, particularly given Pennsylvania's proximity to the conflict in the Ohio Country, and he reacted swiftly. At Campbell's direction, exiles who voiced complaints about their treatment were rounded up and thrown into the city jail on Walnut Street.

Anne often walked the bleak and cold city streets to Southeast Square to visit the grave of Germain and the other exiles who died in Pennsylvania. She thought of the rest of the family: her parents, her many siblings, her nieces and nephews, her uncles, aunts, and cousins. She hoped their luck had been better than hers. Maybe the other cities were nicer and they were gradually building new lives for themselves, or maybe they had made it back home and were enjoying a hot bowl of mutton stew beside the fire, waiting for her to return.

CHAPTER FIVE

Jean Baptiste

It was difficult to feel lucky stuck in the filthy hold of a ship, but Jean Baptiste did. In his thirty years he had never seen such chaos, but when they were waiting to be loaded on the ships at Grand Pré, he and his wife, Marie, had stuck together, ending up on either the *Sarah and Molly* or the *Endeavour*. His sister Cécile and her family were among those they shared the hold with. The rest of his Grand Pré family—his brothers Jacques and Bénoni, his sisters Anne and Madeleine, and his parents, François and Jeanne—had been put aboard other ships. He had no idea what had become of the rest of his siblings and their families.

For seventeen days, he and Marie shared the dismal rations they were given: tough salt pork and flour. They suffered storms together, face to face in the black bottom of their floating prison. The ship stopped once at Boston, where the crew picked out a few of the deportees and removed them from the ship. The air warmed as the days passed. Smells of human waste and rotting flesh ripened and split the air. After nearly three weeks of enduring travel below deck, their ship's anchor finally dropped for good. They had arrived at Hampton Roads, Virginia, their final destination.

Hampton Roads derived the name from its position at the confluence of three major rivers that drain into Chesapeake Bay: the James, the Elizabeth, and the Nansemond. A roadstead (or roads) is a body of water sheltered from currents and ocean swell. Hampton Roads was one of the finest harbours in British North America. Upriver was Jamestown, Britain's first permanent settlement, founded in 1607. Slightly inland was Williamsburg, the stately capital of the Virginia colony. Virginia was then a vast tract of chartered land spanning from the Great Lakes in the north to the known limits of the western frontier. The lieutenant-governor of Virginia, Robert Dinwiddie, was ostensibly second-in-command to Governor John Campbell—who, like most governors, was rarely in the colony he theoretically administered. Dinwiddie was the administrator who would ultimately decide the fate of the Acadian prisoners brought to his shore. But Charles Lawrence had not thought to warn Dinwiddie that fifteen hundred Acadians were on their way, and like Robert Morris in Pennsylvania, Dinwiddie didn't know what to do with them. So at first he did nothing.

At the time of Jean Baptiste's arrival, Virginia was entangled in the war in Ohio Country. The French forts in the Ohio River Valley that so irked the British stood within disputed territory. England claimed the land the forts occupied was part of the vast Virginia colony, while France insisted that they were well within lands the French had claimed nearly a century earlier. In 1754 Dinwiddie had decided to act on the British claim. He called on a promising young Virginian officer named George Washington to lead a military force into the valley and establish a British presence. Dinwiddie personally had much to gain from the move. He had invested money in the Ohio Company, the speculation firm that would directly benefit if Britain could dominate trade in the region. In exploiting his political sway to further his private interests, Dinwiddie was far from unique.

Washington had just turned twenty-two when he headed west into the thick forests of Ohio Country in 1754 on what would become a historic mission into the colonial hinterland. With his plump cheeks and cropped dark hair barely sticking out from under a three-point hat, he looked a mere boy. This was not his first foray west. Two years earlier, when he was just twenty, Washington had marched to the same region to demand that the French vacate the land. They refused. This time, he would accept nothing less than compliance.

When his force of three hundred men learned of a French patrol advancing south from Fort Duquesne, still under construction in 1754, Washington decided to set up an ambush. Sixty-two miles from the fort, Washington's forces surprised the patrol and killed their commander, Joseph Coulon de Villiers de Jumonville. After the attack, Washington retreated and began construction on a British fort. Weeks later, French soldiers surrounded him and his men. Washington surrendered and returned to Virginia. He could not have anticipated that his short-lived effort to assert Britain's authority in the valley would spark a decade of brutal violence known as the Seven Years War or, in the United States, the French and Indian War. The French began fortifying their position, and the British plotted a massive invasion under the leadership of the newly anointed commander-in-chief Edward Braddock.

When the Acadian exiles arrived at Hampton Roads in 1755, they received no warmer a welcome than the exiles had in Boston or Pennsylvania. By now, Jean Baptiste and his fellow

exiles were starving. Lawrence had ordered the prison ships
to be provisioned before departure with "five pounds of flour
and one pound of pork for (each) seven days for each person
so embarked." Based on this, their sloop had probably been
supplied with just enough rations to last the anticipated four- to
six-day journey to the Virginian coast. But it had taken them
seventeen days to reach Hampton Roads. Divided equally (and
it probably wasn't), Jean Baptiste would have consumed less than
six hundred calories per day, and they might well have run out
of food long before the ship's hold was finally opened.

After seventeen days of such a deficient diet, Jean Baptiste
would have started to feel the effects of starvation. Fat is the first
to go. Depending on how much fat the body has stored before
starvation begins, this stage can last for several weeks. When
the body runs out of fat to consume, it begins to break down
its own tissue for energy. Large muscles, the body's final source
of protein, rapidly diminish. The starving person becomes
notably withdrawn and apathetic. Hallucinations are common.
Skin hangs from the body like wet laundry on a line. The sharp
outline of bones presses through the thinning skin, as if the
skeleton were trying to escape. Vital organs shrink and cease to
function normally. The bowels harden and shut down. Death
usually comes from infection or cardiac arrest.

When the ship finally dropped anchor at Hampton Roads,
Jean Baptiste might well have hoped that soon they would be
on shore, feasting at a table and awaiting deeds to new lands.
But Dinwiddie's dithering kept the exiles on-board much longer
than anyone could have imagined.

Dinwiddie's council didn't want the Acadians to settle in the
colony, but council members also recognized that they couldn't

leave the prisoners in the harbour to rot. Dinwiddie wrote to friends in England, notably George Montagu-Dunk, 2nd Earl of Halifax, and Thomas Robinson, the Secretary of State for the Southern Department, lamenting his lack of options. He wrote to Robinson, "It is not the least reasonable to give them lands on our frontiers, where the French and their Indians are robbing and murdering our people."

A representative of the colonial assembly visited the Acadians to inform them of the conditions for their admission to Virginia and to extract an oath of allegiance from them. The Acadians refused the oath, arguing that they remained bound by the oath they'd sworn twenty years earlier to the governor of Nova Scotia. They would "cheerfully submit" to the laws of the colony and live as peaceful subjects, they said, provided they were allowed to practise their religion and to access Catholic priests. Dinwiddie scoffed at their rebuttal, on the grounds that it would violate Virginia's constitution. He also refused to allow the exiles to leave the miserable conditions on the ships, but he did agree to pay for provisions to keep the prisoners alive while a new plan was concocted. It was too late for Jean Baptiste's wife, Marie. At some point during the cold winter months that followed Dinwiddie's decision, she died, hungry and cold, locked beneath the deck of a floating prison in a foreign harbour. If her body wasn't simply dumped over the side, she was likely ferried ashore and buried without ceremony in a pauper's grave.

Provisioning the exiles (those who survived) over the winter had depleted Virginia's coffers, and it was time to make a decision. Dinwiddie reasoned that since Lawrence hadn't told him the Acadians were coming, he could simply refuse to accept them and pass the burden to some other unknowing officer.

With unanimous support from the council, 299 prisoners set sail for Great Britain on a high tide in late May. The rest followed in three other ships shortly after. Dinwiddie may have watched them go and felt satisfied that he'd fulfilled his duty.

An east to west crossing of the Atlantic took an average of thirty days in the eighteenth century. From Hampton Roads, the ships would have sailed into the Gulf Stream and used the current to propel them north. With a broad reach, keeping the wind to the starboard or port rear quarter, the captains could track a relatively straight line across the vast ocean to the south coast of Ireland and the entrance to the English Channel. Jean Baptiste had been a prisoner for almost seven months and was unlikely to be in any shape for a lengthy transatlantic voyage. Conditions must have been favourable because the *Bobby Goodrich*, the vessel Jean Baptiste was on, landed at the port city of Southampton during the last week of June. (The three other transports that left Virginia also made it safely, each landing at a different port. Acadians were disembarked at Liverpool, Bristol, and Falmouth.)

Dinwiddie hadn't bothered to let anyone in authority know that the Acadians were coming. But a Bristol-based mercantile firm, Lidderdale, Harmer and Farrell, heard from one of their ships that a small convoy of transports containing a large number of "Neutral French" was bound for England. The firm contacted the Secretary of State and was promised that the medical department of the Admiralty, the body responsible for prisoners of war, would "take care of the said Neutrals."

Industry crowded Southampton's waterfront. Tall stacks coughed black clouds skyward and pulleys creaked under heavy loads. The salty air rang with commotion. After decades of strife, wars, and stagnation, England was on the rise. Steam engines powered machines once driven by donkeys and men. Coal replaced charcoal in the nation's foundries. The Royal Navy was rapidly expanding, and shipbuilding kept Southampton busy. The first signs of a shift from rural to urban life began to surface. City folk gathered at coffee houses to sip imported drinks and converse, and the cobbled streets seemed alive with people.

But Jean Baptiste and the other exiles did not disembark at Southampton, at least not right away. The *Bobby Goodrich* first landed at Portsmouth Harbour, roughly eighteen miles down the coast from Southampton. There the prisoners were housed in a dank barn on the water's edge and given straw bales and firewood. It was here the virus took hold, smallpox again.

Three days after they arrived, the first person died. More deaths soon followed. They had likely become infected while still on the ship. Those who had already contracted and survived the virus were immune, but the disease spread quickly through the ranks of weakened exiles confined in close quarters. Some of the adults among them wrote to the Admiralty in protest and desperation. They wrote of the "very bad barn, where there is hardly a chimney and no water to be had." They described "a great number of sick persons and also young people of both sexes all together in a lodging where there is neither separation nor distinction of rooms." Soon after the Admiralty received the letter, the group was moved to a somewhat better warehouse in Southampton, where they could suffer in relative comfort.

The exiles on the ship sent to Bristol, the *Virginia Packet*, met with a similarly inauspicious reception. Their ship was towed up the River Avon from the mouth of Severn Estuary, where it tied up at Bristol's quay and sat for five days. The Admiralty had yet to find a place to house the Acadians. The *Bristol Journal*, the city's daily newspaper, reported that on the last Saturday in June "three hundred, a great part of whom are women and children," landed at the city, and on Thursday "were removed to Guinea street."

Guinea Street sat to the southeast of the main quay. The street's drafty depots, bustling sugar refineries, and captain's houses were all situated under the shadow of Bristol's imposing Gothic church, St. Mary Redcliffe. A lightning strike had sliced off its spire in the fifteenth century, but even without it, the massive structure must have been an intimidating symbol of Protestant dominance to the newly arrived Catholic exiles.

The Admiralty had tried to find private homes for the prisoners but encountered "a very strong aversion among all the inhabitants to take these poor wretches in." While the group of nearly three hundred waited on-board the ship at the quay, officials found an empty warehouse near St. Mary Redcliffe and set about turning it into a makeshift prison. Bales of straw were carted down to the Guinea Street warehouse and bars were affixed to the firepits. Then, under a small guard of constables, the Acadians were led through the streets, their meagre possessions loaded in wagons behind them. The exiles likely gawked at the pubs and shops, prostitutes, and even the occasional sub-Saharan African person. The port was a major slaving hub:

Joseph Holbrook, a resident of Guinea Street at the time, had lost one of his slaves and offered a handsome reward for whoever found and returned him. Louis Guigner, the Admiralty official who oversaw the move, reported that the exiles settled into the makeshift prison with a "promise to behave well."

Within three weeks of the Acadians' arrival in Bristol, over sixty cases of smallpox among them had been reported to the Admiralty. At first the sick were quarantined in a small rented house that was turned into a hospital, but as the virus spread the sick and the well were forced to share the same space. The disease also spread through the Acadian exiles in Liverpool and Falmouth. By the end of July, almost a quarter of the nearly one thousand Acadians in England were ill. One doctor advised the Admiralty that the pox "will take its progress through the greater part, if not all of them." Another wrote, "Nothing could be done by way of physic while so many lay wallowing in the same place, infecting each other with their mutual stench and effluvia."

Jean Baptiste watched those he had shared a prison with, since the day they left Grand Pré, toss in agony on straw bales soaked with their sweat, grasping their stomachs, their faces covered in painful blisters that split and oozed pus. Perhaps he wondered why he was spared. The epidemic didn't wane until October. It was almost a year now since the Acadian deportees were forced onto the ships in the Minas Basin. Of the fifteen hundred who set sail for Virginia, only around six hundred were still alive.

The Admiralty had already told the exiles that they would not be permitted to work. Local politicians were keen to "prevent the Clamor of the laboring people in the towns they resided."

Instead the prisoners were given a small allowance of sixpence per day per adult (children received half that). A sixpence coin was equivalent to one fortieth of a pound sterling. Converting eighteenth-century currency to contemporary Canadian values is tricky, but a sixpence in 1756 would be equivalent to about six dollars today. Given their status akin to prisoners of war, the exiles were supplied with daily food. Their cash allowance was to cover all their other needs, such as clothing, bedding, coal, and firewood. Though their freedom of movement was heavily restricted, the exiles were allowed to leave the warehouse to purchase goods when they needed them. If they strayed too far or were found drunk and were reported to the Admiralty, they would lose this privilege.

It might seem that the Acadians sent to England lived in better conditions than those exiled to the American colonies. This likely was not the case. Life in England in the middle of the eighteenth century was difficult for most people and particularly so for impoverished French-speakers dependent on a public allowance. In a hierarchical society strictly divided by class, life on the lower rungs was dirty, hard, and often short-lived. Labourers and craftspeople worked hard to secure their next meal and were subject to the foulest aspects of life. Streets were littered with waste and effluent, both animal and human. Tanneries filled the air with the noxious scents of urine, animal dung, and heavy chemicals. Coal and oil made the air dark and sooty, coating surfaces with a thick black sludge. The districts nearest the water in port cities were often the filthiest, home to the dirtiest industries. Crime was rampant, and punishments were severe. In 1688, only fifty types of crime carried a death sentence; that number increased steadily over the decades of the eighteenth century, until no fewer than 220 crimes were punished with death. The theft of a piece of cutlery or an article of clothing could end at the gallows or in transportation to the colonies. It was in these wretched conditions that the vast majority of the urban-dwelling poor lived and worked. Not surprisingly, it is also where the Acadian exiles were sent.

Life in England began to blur for Jean Baptiste. Without work or purpose, the days melted together. The squalor of port industry consumed his daily life. Bound to his small district and with nothing to do, he could only exist, trapped in a system that was designed to keep him from achieving anything. Threats to survival lurked around every corner. The port cities of England were dangerous places for the destitute. Average life expectancy for males hovered around age thirty-five at the time, and for good reasons: bad water, scarce food supply, terrible working conditions, inaccessible health care, and virulent disease.

The only source of strength left to the Acadians was their community. With that in mind, Jean Baptiste found comfort. Marie had died a world away, and though memories of his past life with her surely lingered, his old life must have felt distant. And with his new circumstances came another hope. By the time they landed in England, Britain and France had officially declared war against one another, making the Acadian exiles prisoners of war. Rumours circulated among them that the French government had asked the British Admiralty to free the exiles and send them to France, where they would be given land and allowed to work in the fields again—part of a prisoner trade common in times of war. Jean Baptiste and a woman his age named Marguerite Célestin dit Bellemère, also an exile from Grand Pré, married, albeit without the benefit of a priest or a church. Perhaps they toasted not only their marriage but also the prospect of a new life in France. Even in a warehouse prison in England, apparently, it was possible to believe in the future.

CHAPTER SIX

Joseph

Joseph and Marie-Josèphe had packed quickly, taking only what they could carry. They were not the only ones in Cobeguit in 1751 to come to the decision to flee. The whole community had decided to leave. Nestled between Grand Pré and Beaubassin, Cobeguit afforded its residents a view of just how many British soldiers were pouring into the region. Perhaps Joseph wrote to his family in Pisiguit and Grand Pré to urge them to follow his lead, even though he knew he couldn't wait for them to reply. Marie-Josèphe's parents, Ambroise and Élisabeth Bourg, were leaving early the next day, determined to walk just over thirty miles to the banks of the Mer Rogue and then sail the short distance to the French territory of Île Saint-Jean. Joseph and his wife would go with them. For years, Abbé Jean-Louis Le Loutre had been spreading word around Acadia about how good life was on Île Saint-Jean: plenty of land, fertile soil, good weather—and no red-coated soldiers. The community had decided together to depart. Although there was no immediate danger—the British were not yet knocking on their doors—they prepared to leave with the haste of a scared and intimidated populace. If any particular factor hastened their departure, it may have been the fact that French ships were providing free transportation to those willing to make the trek across the strait to the island. France was keenly interested in populating Île Saint-Jean, but the offer wouldn't stand forever. Le Loutre likely tipped off the elders of Cobeguit to the plan during one of his travelling sermons. Maybe it was the push they needed to pack up their whole town and leave.

The first part of the extended Bourg/LeBlanc clan's journey to the coast took them through thick forests and hilly terrain. Joseph had spent his life on the banks of the Minas Basin. Here on the high plateau of the interior (where the stretch of the Trans-Canada Highway known as the Cobequid Pass now runs), the terrain was different. The omnipresent sound of the water in the bay didn't muffle all other sounds. Unfamiliar birdsong seemed louder in the crisp air. The wind cut through the tree-tops with a high whistle. The trek likely took the group the better part of a week, with young and old needing frequent stops to rest. Joseph's youngest child, Bénoni, only two, was probably carried most of the way on his mother's back, wrapped tight so as to not fall out during the steep descents of the forested hills. His three older siblings—Joseph, age seven; Simon Joseph, age eleven; and Ambroise, age fourteen—also struggled with the terrain.

Joseph and Marie-Josèphe tried to keep the children's spirits up with talk of the ship they would take across the channel. Joseph spent his life on the land, but as a child in Grand Pré he had gone fishing with his father and one of his brothers. In a tiny single-mast punt with scant room for the three of them, he and his brother would man the lines while they caught as many writhing fish as they could, careful not to crush any under the sturdy heels of their boots. Perhaps he would be able to take his own sons fishing once they were settled in Île Saint-Jean.

At long last they crested the final hill, and they could see the waiting ships.

The influx of British soldiers and fortifications that prompted Joseph's family and the rest of the residents of Cobeguit to flee in 1751 were a result of a change in colonial leadership in Halifax. Governor Phillips, with whom Acadian deputies had brokered an oath of neutrality in 1730, and who had overseen the colony from his cozy manor in London ever since, was gone. The man who was commissioned to take his place was far less of a diplomat than his predecessor. Edward Cornwallis landed in the colony of Nova Scotia in 1749 to take over as governor. Son of Charles, 4th Baron Cornwallis, young Edward started service at the age of twelve as a royal page to King George I. His first taste of war came at the Battle of Fontenoy in 1745, during the War of the Austrian Succession, when the French forces decimated Cornwallis's large regiment, killing at least four hundred of the men under his personal command. He had more success putting down the Jacobites in Scotland. After fighting on the winning side at the Battle of Culloden, Cornwallis led a group of soldiers on a wholesale slaughter of anyone suspected of supporting Bonnie Prince Charlie's cause. They rounded up farmers, blacksmiths, cobblers, women, and children, locked them in their houses, and burned it all to the ground. They called this the pacification of the Highlands. Having proved his willingness to quell an unruly population with violence, Cornwallis was rewarded with the governorship of Nova Scotia.

Cornwallis's first task was to establish a base of operations to protect Britain's colonial interests. He chose a spot with a usable harbour and a defensible hill and named the new settlement after George Montagu-Dunk, 2nd Earl of Halifax. With a stronghold under construction, Cornwallis turned his attention to asserting Britain's dominance in the region. On paper, Britain had controlled the land since 1713, but in reality, the nearly fifteen thousand Acadians outnumbered the few hundred British in the colony by a ratio of twenty-five to one. Cornwallis commissioned forts and garrisons across the region. Soldiers poured in from England to man them. Other English settlers arrived in Halifax, which quickly grew into a town.

Abbé Le Loutre had been warning Acadian community leaders for years that they and their people needed to leave the colony of Nova Scotia and move to French territory. Le Loutre thought that if the Acadians of Chignecto moved to the other side of the Missaguash River, they'd be safe in French territory. Instead, the Acadians who opted to leave Chignecto headed for Île Saint-Jean. Perhaps they believed that the geographical separation of an island would put them outside Britain's reach. Between 1750 and 1753, nearly a third of the Acadian inhabitants of Nova Scotia relocated to Île Saint-Jean, and the island's population swelled to nearly five thousand people.

The island had sat sparsely populated by settlers since Jacques Cartier first laid eyes on its sandy red shoreline in 1534. Though France laid claim to the island as part of Acadia in 1604, few Europeans settled on Île Saint-Jean. The island's primary inhabitants were the Mi'kmaq, who called the island Epekwitk. They had lived there for thousands of years, and though they welcomed the French as trading partners and established a mutually beneficial relationship almost entirely free of conflict, they never recognized France's land claim. For decades after European settlement the island was little more than a rugged outpost for a few French soldiers and a handful of settler families. Only when conflict over Acadia increased between the French and British did significant numbers of Acadians begin to view Île Saint-Jean as an attractive option for refuge.

When Joseph and his family arrived on the island—they likely landed at Pointe-Prime, near what is now Charlottetown, the capital of Prince Edward Island—they found a mixture of Mi'kmaq inhabitants, settlers and soldiers from France, and Acadians like themselves who had relocated to the island at various times in the preceding three decades. On Île Royale, nothing grew in the rocky soil around Louisbourg, and bringing in goods from Québec and France had proven expensive. France hoped the rich red soil of Île Saint-Jean would become the breadbasket for its Maritime possessions. Anyone willing to seize the opportunity received free passage and free land.

Île Saint-Jean was mostly flat and pretty. Tight stands of forest knitted the east and west together; the Hillsborough River was the seam. To the west of the river, the island was windswept and pitted with shallow bays that reached inland from the north and south, almost touching in some places. The far western lands were nearly barren—long sandy beaches trimmed the shoreline, and iron-orange sandbars shadowed most of the coast just offshore. East of the river were rolling hills, gentle valleys, and glens. The forests were taller and darker here. Across the northern fringe of the island stretched towering sand dunes wearing crowns of fescue and kelp. On the island's east coast, the land dropped off. The shore was jagged and rocky. Bays and promontories marked the coastline, and the soil blazed red, nearly the colour of glazed clay, reminiscent of the marshy soil of the Minas Basin.

The newcomers settled all across the island. Joseph and Marie-Josèphe along with a handful of other families chose a small plot in Havre de la Fortune, a handsome bay on the east coast. Joseph might have found the similarly coloured soil a comforting reminder of home, a sign that he would be able to provide for his family as he had in Cobeguit. Most farmers on the island grew oats and grain and kept livestock. According to the 1752 census, Joseph had sowed four bushels of wheat, and he owned four oxen, six cows, five calves, one horse, six pigs, and fourteen chickens.

The fertile soil would have made for an agricultural paradise if not for the plagues. First, in 1749, came the black field mice, inky balls that ravaged the island and ate the year's harvest. Louisbourg had to send emergency rations to keep everyone alive. The following year, locusts came, blackening the sky in hordes of hundreds of millions, devouring swathes of crops and forest as they razed the island like a highly organized army. Again the harvest was destroyed, and again Louisbourg had to come to the settlers' rescue. In 1751, the year Joseph and his family arrived, the island experienced a terrible drought.

Those three years turned the island into a barren place. One census taker described the conditions. "They subsisted on the shell fish they gathered on the shores of the harbour when the tide was out," Sieur de la Roque wrote. "The greatest number amongst them had not even bread to eat." The following year, Father Jacques Girard, a priest who had come to the island from

Cobeguit, noted that many of the recently arrived Acadians had no clothes. "Most of the children are entirely naked," he reported, "and when I go into a house they are crouched in the ashes, close to the fire."

Life on the island was hard, harder than Joseph could have imagined. And when Charles Lawrence issued his deportation order in 1755, the Acadians on Île Saint-Jean realized that they couldn't return to the mainland, even if they wanted to.

News of the chaos trickled across the strait. Families who had fled ahead of the deportation spread word of what was happening. When Joseph heard the news, he must have known this meant that his parents, his siblings, and their families had been stripped of their homes and their livelihoods and deported from the land where they had toiled for so many years. But then a different type of report began making its way through the Acadian communities of Île Saint-Jean: the French and their Indigenous allies were fighting the British, and they were winning. In 1757, in the British colony of New York, six thousand French and nearly two thousand Indigenous warriors attacked Fort William Henry. They caught the British unprepared. The fort's commander quickly raised the white flag after cannons obliterated the fort's northwestern wall. The French seized all the British ammunition and sent the captives south. Frustrated soldiers and warriors, denied the battle they'd come prepared to wage, descended on the retreating column in a frenzy of brutality and hacked away at the unprotected line.

The fall of Fort William Henry was only the latest victory for the French. Since the loss of Beauséjour, they had experienced success across the Ohio Valley and along the lakes of New York, first at Fort Duquesne and then at Fort Bull and Fort Oswego.

And in Acadia, supposedly a secure British possession, the Acadian militia were mounting a determined resistance. When Joseph heard about the fighting, he decided to leave his wife and children in Havre de la Fortune and return to Chignecto. The decision was difficult. His wife was pregnant, and he would be leaving the hard work of farming in the hands of his oldest sons, now approaching adulthood. Only a powerful need to avenge the wrongs done to his family, to his people, could have propelled him back. He was not alone. Nearly every refugee on the island had left behind family in Acadia, relations who had, in all likelihood, long been expelled and sent into the unknown. They didn't have a chance to stand their ground in 1755, when the deportations started. They were caught unaware, or, like Joseph, were far from home when the Expulsion began. But now it was time to fight.

Like all resistance movements, it started underground, hidden in pockets across the region. Small groups, with the help of Mi'kmaq warriors, had been raiding forts and villages across Acadia since the turn of the century. Every time the British committed an act of aggression against a French community, the militia would appear and push back. They resisted the British at the Fortress of Louisbourg, when the British first attacked it in the 1740s. They appeared again in Grand Pré to harry Fort Vieux Logis. And they descended several times on Dartmouth, just across the harbour from Halifax, taking prisoners and causing chaos.

Charles Deschamps de Boishébert et de Raffetot, a military officer born in Québec, arrived in Acadie Française in 1746. In concert with a militia consisting of Acadian fighters and Wabanaki Confederacy warriors, he helped fortify the Saint

John River Valley and Miramachi and participated in the ongoing campaign to terrorize British settlements, instill fear among settlers, and push back against the ever-increasing British military presence in Acadia. The militia would sneak into settlements at night, capture soldiers, burn buildings, and disappear back into the woods before a defence could be mounted against them. Boishébert joined with Abbé Le Loutre, who had been a militia leader during the six-year conflict with the British that would become known as Father Le Loutre's War, prominent Acadian resistance leader Joseph Broussard, and several other determined leaders. By the time Joseph returned to Acadia, possibly to join the resistance, the group had grown in size and become much more organized.

The militia operated like all guerilla groups, using fear to compensate for its small size and lack of equipment. After the deportations began in 1755, the militia commandeered British supply ships on the Mer Rouge and raided British forts and warehouses across Acadia. In April 1757, the resistance attacked a warehouse in Pisiguit, burned it to the ground, and killed thirteen soldiers. However, soldiers weren't the only targets, and fear settled like a thick fog across the region. British settlers were afraid to go out. A trip to the well for water could cost someone their scalp.

A sharp knife worked best, but in a pinch, a piece of slate or a broken oyster shell would suffice. With a firm grip on the hair, the scalper sliced two semi-circular lines around the top of the skull, usually following the hairline as reference. That was the delicate part. Then came the pulling. Using the hair as leverage, the scalper lifted the flesh from the skull like an orange peel. Sometimes the victim was dead before the scalping began, but not always. Scalping was not in and of itself fatal. The scalp's connective tissue isn't deep, and it contains far fewer blood vessels than other parts of the body. It was possible to survive a scalping, but most did not. Scalps were trophies, proof of a kill. Both the French and British engaged in the brutal practice and even offered to pay cash for the scalps of their enemies. First Cornwallis and then Lawrence placed bounties on Mi'kmaw scalps—any Mi'kmaw scalp. Male scalps were worth ten guineas in 1752—Lawrence raised the reward in 1756 to twenty-five pounds (roughly twenty-six guineas)—a significant sum, but the scalps of women and children also had value. Officially, the bounty applied only to Mi'kmaw scalps, but it's doubtful those responsible for accepting the scalps and paying the rewards put much effort in to determining provenance. Some of the scalps exchanged for cash may well have come from the dark-haired and olive-complected Acadians.

The militia's tactics succeeded. Fear spread like a virus through the ranks of the British soldiers stationed across Nova Scotia. One young man confided his constant state of dread to a colleague. "I expect at every moment to be swallowed up by the French and Indians," he wrote, "and we dare not stray out of our lines for fear of losing our scalps." The Protestant settlers who had laid claim to the Acadian lands questioned their decision to move to such a violent place. Lieutenant John Knox, the leader of an Irish regiment sent to relieve the weary troops at Fort Cumberland, arrived just in time to witness the effect of the militia's terror. One night, a sentry heard a rustle in the bushes and opened fire with his rifle. The rest of the guard followed suit, unloading their weapons wildly into the dark. The British were likely equipped with smooth-muzzle long rifles, which were inaccurate and unpredictable. Spiral-muzzle rifles, which spun the bullets, would have resulted in improved accuracy, but few if any of these rifles would have been in Nova Scotia at the time. Instead, the British fired and essentially sprayed the shot in the general direction they were pointing—if the rifle fired at all. By the time the officers had stopped the shooting, several soldiers were wounded—British soldiers. Knox called it an episode of "impetuous firing of their own comrades," or what's now referred to as friendly fire.

Knox had unknowingly walked into a war zone. The militia controlled the forests and the marshlands. The British stayed in their forts. Knox wrote in 1757, "We were said to be Masters of the province of Nova Scotia, or Acadia, which, however, was only an imaginary possession." Though the militia had succeeded in spreading fear throughout the region, it came at a cost. Each skirmish with the British claimed Acadian lives as well. On a cold wet December morning near the British fort at Annapolis Royal in 1757, a detachment of British soldiers and armed men from the community went in search of prisoners who had been out gathering firewood when the militia had taken them days earlier. While the rescue group members were fording a river on a narrow wooden bridge, they were fired on from the forest. The British commander was shot and his men retreated, shooting blindly into the trees as they fled. According to one British soldier taken prisoner who later escaped to Fort Cumberland, the attackers had suffered sixteen causalities during the raid. Though the militia had the element of surprise, the Expulsion had drastically reduced their Acadian numbers, and each life lost during an ambush depleted their force still further. The British could easily bring in more soldiers, but the militia had a harder time recruiting. France was too busy with the ever-growing war to consider sending reinforcements. The militia was on its own and fighting an uphill battle.

Reports of the dangers in Acadia made Marie-Josèphe question Joseph's decision, but she and their children needed to survive. Their struggling farm, as reported in the 1752 census, would have barely fed a family of eight, even if growing conditions had improved over the years. Even with the oldest sons working in the fields and caring for the animals, life would be worse without Joseph.

Havre de la Fortune sat in the wind. Cold, salty air whipped off the Gulf of St. Lawrence and slammed into the shoreline in fall and winter. It stunted the trees and yellowed the fields. (The dwarf forests that ring the bays on this part of the island are known still as Acadian forests.) By 1757, Cobeguit was a field of ash presided over by a small fort full of red coats. The war between England and France had spread across most of Europe and North America. Frederick II (later known as Frederick the Great), leader of the powerful German kingdom of Prussia, had sided with Britain, and Prussian troops were fighting against the allied armies of France, Austria, Russia, and Sweden for control of central Europe.

The Acadians on Île Saint-Jean were safe if the soil beneath their feet remained French, but as the eighteenth century's middle decade drew to a close, fortune began to favour the British. What would happen to the people on the island if the British invaded and succeeded in driving out the French? Boishébert and the militia had established refugee camps on the Miramichi River and the Baie des Chaleurs, and for years the fishermen of Malpec on the northwest coast of the island had been ferrying destitute families to the camps. Of those who went though, most came back; conditions in the camps were even worse than on the island. But if the British invaded, this was one escape route.

Marie-Josèphe knew about the camps and the boats that left from Malpec, but she could not bear the thought of leaving, not without her husband. She had seven children and an eighth on the way. As the wind blew down from the north and glazed the wheat fields with ice, Marie-Josèphe waited for Joseph's return. Her wait would be in vain. She did not know that Joseph lay dead in Cobeguit. How he died is unknown. He may have been among the countless lost during the resistance's fight for Acadia. Marie-Joséphe would wait nearly a year for him. By then it must have been clear to her that he was not coming back. She and her children, including her newborn son, Georges-Robert, needed to flee Île Saint-Jean before it, and they, fell into the hands of the British.

CHAPTER SEVEN

Marie & Josette

Marie Thibodeau, née LeBlanc — Joseph's sister and closest sibling in age (she was just two years older) — would have understood her sister-in-law Marie-Joséphe's fears all too well, for she had lived for over five years on the run from the British.

Marie had spent the first thirty years of her life in Grand Pré. She was the fourth of François and Jeanne's twelve children and the second oldest girl after her sister Anne. She grew up helping her mother raise the rest of the brood. The youngest were fifteen years her junior, and for them she might have been more of a mother figure than a sister. In 1727, she married Jean Baptiste Thidodeau dit Cramatte. *Dit* (said) indicates a nickname used in place of the original surname, a practice intended to help distinguish between different people bearing identical names, which was common when families were large, intermarriage inevitable, and sons were named to honour fathers, grandfathers, and uncles. Nicknames were often used in the French military to separate an enlisted man from his former identity. Chosen nicknames could reflect familial origin or occupation, but the origin of *Cramatte* is unclear. Marie and Jean Baptiste married in the church of Saint-Charles-des-Mines, just a month shy of her seventeenth birthday.

We can't be certain exactly who was with Marie as she pushed deeper and deeper into Acadie Française. It is probably safe to assume that her youngest children, aged seven and nine, accompanied her. According to a surviving letter, her daughter Marguerite Josèphe, Marie's oldest child and already married, was likely also part of the group. The families found stability in the Saint John River Valley, probably near the community of Pointe-Sainte-Anne (now Fredericton, the capital of New Brunswick).

The valley had become a refuge for Acadians fleeing the British in 1755, as it had sixty-five years earlier after the fall of Port-Royal. Pointe-Sainte-Anne, then known as Fort Nashwaak, was made the provisional capital of Acadia in 1690 while French officials sorted out how to recapture Port-Royal. The fort sat farther upriver than many of the original Acadian settlements found on its banks, settled throughout the later decades of the seventeenth century. After the death of Commandant Joseph Robinau de Villebon in 1700, the French abandoned Fort Nashwaak. Unlike Grand Pré, the riverside settlements struggled to attract immigrants, at least until the British took over Acadia in 1713. Acadians fleeing British control eventually made their way to the former site of Fort Nashwaak to establish Point-Sainte-Anne.

It was to places like Pointe-Sainte-Anne that Abbé Le Loutre had been advising his parishioners to flee in the years leading up to the Expulsion. Marie decided, like her siblings Joseph and Josette, to heed Le Loutre's call, but instead of heading to Île Saint-Jean and Île Royale, she followed many other Acadians from the Chignecto region who packed up their possessions and crossed the Missaguash River into French territory before 1755. Perhaps they thought being closer to Québec would be safer than settlement on the islands, or maybe they knew that the Acadian militia had based its operations out of the valley for years and made the area relatively safe.

Joseph Godin dit Bellefontaine dit Beausejour was born and raised near Fort Nashwaak, on a riverside acreage given to his father by Commandant Villebon. The son of an interpreter who worked closely with the Wabanaki Confederacy, Godin assisted his father from an early age, quickly picked up local Indigenous languages, knew the local geography well, and had earned the trust of the Wəlastəkwiyik, Abenaki, and Mi'kmaq. He was an ideal candidate for a leadership role, and in 1749, Boishébert appointed him commander of the local militia. Godin was determined that the British would never take his homeland from him and his people. His leadership was immediately put to the test.

Lawrence knew of the militia's activity in the valley and was keen to wipe it out. Between 1748 and 1755, the British sent three separate expeditions up the river to attack Acadian communities and destroy Boishébert's forts. The Acadians repelled them each time, though not without cost. Days before the 1755 attack, Boishébert, knowing he was outnumbered, burned Fort Menagoueche at the mouth of the river and then fled into the woods. With Menagoueche gone, the British returned to Fort Cumberland to plan yet another attack. Fortunately for Godin and Boishébert, the Expulsion and battles elsewhere pulled British attention away from the Saint John River Valley. For the next few years, Acadian refugees who made their way to the valley found a safe haven.

The river valley was a new world to Marie, remarkably different than the tidal salt flats of the Minas Basin. The river that cut through the wide, low valley dominated the landscape. The thick forests, full of ancient broadleaf hardwoods, towering red spruce, and white pines, bore little resemblance to the scrawny coastal forests near Grand Pré. The canopy was thick enough to block the sun and allowed a brief respite from the hot dry air of the valley. Her youngest children, Françoise Cécile and Marie Madeleine, were only seven and nine, and they found their new landscape an enchanting wonderland. Marie hoped they'd be able to stay in this place, at least for a while.

The hamlets were humble and discreet. Small clusters of wooden houses and barns were set among the tall forests that lined the river's edge. Though they were safer here than anywhere else, the threat of British warships appearing on the river was a constant fear, and camouflage was an important consideration.

How the Thibodeaus reached the valley and exactly when are difficult to ascertain, for records are sparse. Marie and her husband, Jean Baptiste, had left Grand Pré years before Winslow arrived with the deportation order. First they went to Cobeguit, where perhaps they considered heading to Île Saint-Jean with her brother Joseph and his family. Instead they opted to travel west, into Acadie Française, where they show up in Sieur de la Roque's census of 1752 as refugees located in the community of Aulac, just outside the walls of Fort Beauséjour. They were part of what has become known as the Acadian Exodus, the migration of thousands of Acadians who gave up their homes to travel, often on foot, into French territory, where they hoped they'd be safe from the reach of the British.

Thanks to a brief reference to Jean Baptiste in a letter penned by the infamous spy Thomas Pichon—the most traitorous figure ever to set foot in Acadia—we know that by 1754 the Thibodeau family had left Aulac and travelled farther west to the Saint John River Valley. Born in northwestern France in 1700, Pichon arrived in Acadia in 1752 as a clerk to the then governor of Île Royale, Jean-Louis de Raymond. Pichon, an educated man and a competent writer, felt his position at Louisbourg was beneath him. Disputes with Raymond eventually led to his departure from the fortress, and he was sent to Beauséjour. Though his official position at the border fort was the chief clerk of stores, he quickly gained the confidence of Commandant Vergor and Abbé Le Loutre (the latter was serving as the fort's priest at the time). He helped both men write letters, and in the process Pichon became privy to sensitive and important information about the fort's weaknesses and the movements of the French military, the Acadian militia, and Mi'kmaq warriors.

How Thomas Pichon and George Scott, the commander of Fort Lawrence, came to be acquainted remains a matter of dispute. Much of what is known about Pichon's life comes from his own autobiography and may not be entirely credible. The two men may have met each other when Pichon was employed in Louisbourg. It is also possible they met in one of the local eateries near Fort Beauséjour and Fort Lawrence. (During times of peace, the French and British frequented the same establishments.) Regardless of how their exchange began, between the late summer of 1754 and the following June, Scott paid the ambitious and mercenary Pichon for information about the fort and New France.

In one of the series of letters that Pichon wrote to Scott, he mentioned that he was considering the acquisition of a plot of land near the fort, land that was once owned by Jean Thibodeau, father-in-law to a certain Grandmaison. Pichon noted that he was able to convince Thibodeau to return to Cobeguit, but that Grandmaison left for the Saint John River Valley to meet up with Thibodeau's family, who were living there. The Jean Thibodeau who Pichon referred to was Marie's husband, Jean Baptiste Thibodeau dit Cramatte, and Grandmaison was their son-in-law, Jean Baptiste Guillot dit Grandmaison, husband of their daughter Marguerite-Josèphe. This brief and casual reference revealed that Marie's family, which had once called the region home, was now divided. (It isn't clear when Jean Baptiste Grandmaison made his way to the Saint John River Valley to join his wife and children, but he died in 1795, in Madawaska, near today's border between the provinces of Quebec and New Brunswick. He was likely part of a group of Acadians that moved to Madawaska from the Saint John River Valley in the 1780s.) Pichon focused on an opportunity to enrich himself and gave little thought to the Acadian people whose lives were in a constant state of disruption. But this is to be expected from the man who almost single-handedly delivered Fort Beauséjour into the hands of his nation's enemy in exchange for gold.

Less than two months after Pichon's espionage helped the British take Fort Beauséjour, Monckton began deporting the Acadians who remained in the region. In pursuit of families who at the last minute had made desperate escapes into French territory, Monckton's raiding parties launched an assault in early

September on several small communities on the Petitcodiac River. When the British landed on the western bank of the river (near what is now the town of Hillsborough, south of the city of Moncton) and set fire to over one hundred buildings, the Acadian militia responded. Boishébert, having burned his own fort at the mouth of the Saint John River rather than let it fall into British hands, caught wind of the pending attack. He assembled a large force of Acadian, Mi'kmaq, and Wəlastəkwiyik fighters. The group made its way to the riverbank and ambushed the raiding party. After hours of fighting, the British forces retreated. Twenty-two British soldiers had died. Boishébert had made his stand, but he was only able to push the British away from the western bank. Other raiding parties that had also landed on the eastern side of the river burned, pillaged, and imprisoned all they came across on their way back to Fort Cumberland.

Boishébert and the rest of the militia were emboldened by their victory. For more than fifty years, various groups of organized Acadian and Indigenous fighters had raided British villages and forts and generally resisted the British expansion across Acadia, but this triumph was different. With the fall of Beauséjour and Lawrence's deportation order, they were now at war. Defending the communities along the Petitcodiac River was just the beginning for the wartime resistance fighters. Long after the ships full of Marie's siblings and thousands of other Acadians left for the ports of British America, the Acadian and Mi'kmaw resistance would continue to sneak into British territory and conduct menacing raids on major communities such as Pisiquit, Lawrencetown, Lunenburg, and even Halifax, the capital.

Marie and her family had been fortunate enough to always be one step ahead of the fighting. They made it out of Chignecto before Monckton took control. They'd been far from Petitcodiac when Boishébert pushed the British back, and so far life in the vast green river valley was peaceful. The old days in Grand Pré were forever gone, and although she didn't know it, her life on the run wasn't over yet. Tired of the endless war, Britain was gearing up for its largest assault in North America. What happened next would change everything.

The arrival of the sloop on the Riviére des Habitants was all the warning Josette needed. She'd been dreading this day for three years, ever since the deportations began in 1755 and hungry refugees from Acadia came pouring across the Strait of Canso, the narrow waterway that separated mainland Acadia from Île Royale, telling anyone who would listen that they'd abandoned their homes and fled rather than face exile at the hands of the British. Some were headed for Louisbourg, hoping the fort would keep them safe. Others hoped to settle in the communities to the north, places like Port Toulouse, fearing that the southeast corner, where Josette lived, wasn't far enough away from the chaos brewing on the mainland. Families came through broken and lost: widows with ten or more young children; parents who'd become separated from their children, and children without their parents. Josette dreaded what would happen if the rumours that had been circulating for the past few weeks materialized and the British seized control of the Fortress of Louisbourg. Now, in the late summer of 1758, it seemed that the day had come. The ship dropped anchor past the narrows, near where the calm waters met the sea. The mast was visible from a long way off, its fearsome Union Jack waving proudly in the breeze.

Josette and her husband, Jean Baptiste Landry dit Labbé, had settled in the small hamlet of Rivière aux Habitants seven years earlier with their five small children. Like her brother Joseph and sisters Marguerite and Marie, Josette's husband and his family saw the warning signs of what was to come if they remained in Grand Pré. They chose this place for its proximity to the river, wide, slow, and blue. Low land thickly furnished with short evergreens lined both sides. The river emptied into the Atlantic Ocean at a broad estuary with clear views of the vast expanse beyond. But it wasn't at all like the salt marshes and meadows of Grand Pré. The soil here was thin and non-productive; just below the surface sat long slabs of rock, like those worn bare near the shore.

But the river was a beautiful place, the surrounding land more green than anything in Grand Pré. Here Guillaume Beniost, a man they knew from Grand Pré, had established a sawmill. When word of the Expulsion reached Josette's door, she wept for the family she'd left behind. They'd chosen Île Royale because it was French. They'd hoped the great fortress at Louisbourg would keep them safe. French troops on patrols regularly passed through her small community, and when food was scarce, sometimes they'd bring provisions. The fortress was also a target, Josette realized, and if it fell, then everything would change.

Louisbourg, the jewel in the hilt of France's imperial sword, was the largest fortress in North America and France's most important possession after Québec. It took twenty-eight years to complete. The fortress sat at the end of a narrow peninsula on the rocky northeastern coast of Île Royale. To reach it by land required crossing windswept marshes and low plains. Water surrounded the other three sides: the crashing waves of the Atlantic, the narrow channel that led to a natural harbour, and the harbour itself. More than one hundred cannons and high, thick stone walls protected it. Louisbourg, the colonial headquarters for Île Royale and Île Saint-Jean and the first line of defence against naval attacks heading for the St. Lawrence, had some potentially fatal flaws. First, the soldiers who manned the fortress were lacking in training, skill, and experience. Second, Louisbourg was entirely dependent on food imported from other parts of the French colony. If the British could block Louisbourg's supply lines, those in the fortress would simply starve.

The sight of the sloop on the river signalled that Josette's darkest fears were about to materialize. The siege lasted nearly seven weeks. The British fleet, under the command of Admiral Edward Boscawen, split into three attack groups and attempted to take the fortress the same way they had in 1745, the first time it fell to British hands. Nearly two hundred ships carrying more than fourteen thousand British soldiers converged on the fortress in the first week of June 1758. The British knew that if they tried to attack from the sea, the fortress's many cannons would obliterate the fleet. The land offered its own challenges. The heavy cannons the British would need to blow open the fortress's thick walls could easily sink in the marshes, and the open plains would afford them little protective cover. But in 1745, they had successfully crossed the swamps and forced the French to surrender, and they resolved to repeat history.

Two major units navigated high seas and harsh weather in an attempt to land south of the fortress and begin their march across the swamps. At the same time, Boscawen sent Brigadier General James Wolfe and a contingent of twelve hundred soldiers out into a thick fog with orders to march around the harbour and seize the lighthouse battery. The battery was the fortress's main exterior position and the key to their stronghold over the entrance to the harbour. It sat on a high bluff overlooking the fortress and the island battery, a smaller defensive position located on a small island in the middle of the harbour's mouth. If the British could take control of the lighthouse battery, they could easily destroy the island battery. This would unlock the harbour to the British fleet and virtually guarantee the fortress's defeat.

Wolfe and his forces quickly accomplished their goal, and they aimed their cannons at the island. The soldiers inside Louisbourg's walls were both outnumbered and trapped. Charles Lawrence, who had been promoted to governor of Nova Scotia just two years earlier, was leading one of the attack forces. He brought his soldiers into position in the marshlands, while Brigadier General Edward Whitmore followed suit with his flank. Louisbourg was a tinderbox awaiting a flame.

The spark came in late July, several weeks into the siege. Despite the best efforts of the French, the British artillery line crept closer and closer, until their fire began to reduce the town to rubble. Wolfe forced the small French fleet trapped in the harbour to nearly ground itself as the crews tried to escape the cannon fire. On July 21, a mortar round struck a French warship and set it on fire. Strong winds whisked the flames into the sails of two other ships. The results were disastrous: three-fifths of the French fleet were taken out of commission, and now the fortress was almost entirely surrounded. Days later, cannon fire hit the largest building in the fortress, the military headquarters, burning it to the ground. The French pinned their hopes on a relief fleet sent from France to bolster their numbers and push back against their attackers, but they hoped in vain. The British crushed the fleet before it even left the Mediterranean. Louisbourg, an ocean away from reinforcements, was surrounded, clinging to its rocky stronghold deep in the enemy's territory.

Finally, on July 25, Boscawen ordered the *Pembroke*, a sixty-gun naval ship, to take what was left of the French fleet. With the harbour masked in fog, the *Pembroke* dropped its small boats and entered the harbour. Under-manned and unprepared, the two remaining French vessels were easily seized, as recorded in the *Pembroke*'s logbook by the ship's master, a young James Cook. Arriving in Louisbourg fresh from his first transatlantic voyage, Cook would go on to circumnavigate the world on three separate occasions, charting vast expanses of the Pacific. He also had the distinction of not losing a single member of his crew to scurvy when he circumnavigated from 1768 to 1771.

With lines of provisioning choked off, cannon fire smashing through the courtyards, and the last of the French fleet lost, Augustin de Boschenry de Drucourt, governor of Île Royale and commander of Louisbourg, surrendered. Not long afterward, the French abandoned Fort Duquesne in Ohio Country. Drucourt and his officers would return to France, where they would be given new positions in the navy and live out their remaining days in the relative comfort of home. But for the people left behind, the surrender of Louisbourg would change everything.

The fall of Louisbourg was the most important British victory yet in the Seven Years War. As long as the French had controlled Louisbourg, the British could not safely sail around Île Royale and into the Gulf of St. Lawrence to take the French strongholds of Québec and Montréal—the key to winning North America. With Louisbourg now in their hands, the British could prepare for the final push.

Major General Jeffrey Amherst, who had led the British army during the siege on Louisbourg, wanted to prevent the Acadians from banding together and mounting a resistance to Britain's newly established dominance. He ordered Lieutenant Colonel Andrew Rollo to sail a fleet to Île Saint-Jean, establish a fort, and begin rounding up all the inhabitants. Amherst launched his own troops on a burn-and-pillage campaign across Île Royale. All Acadians would be arrested and brought to the Fortress of Louisbourg, where they would be loaded onto ships.

The Acadians were now fair game for deportation, and the British commanders wasted no time in signing the paperwork to authorize their expulsion. It wouldn't be like the first time. When Lawrence ordered the original deportation, he was able to justify his decision as a removal of a dangerous people from British land. This time, though the British had taken Louisbourg, Britain had not yet won the war, and Île Royale was still French territory. The North American colonies refused to accept any more exiles. England, which still had nearly a thousand Acadians imprisoned among Bristol, Liverpool, and Southampton, didn't want them, either. This time, the British would deport the Acadians to France.

Josette resolved that neither she nor her family would be on one of those ships, even though her youngest child, Madeleine, was only four years old. If they could hide in the thick forests around Rivière aux Habitant until the raiding party swept through their abandoned homes, maybe they could make a break for the coast. Other families were heading to Île Madame, a low island to the northeast. Basque fishermen had been frequenting Île Madame since at least the sixteenth century, and by 1758 it had grown into a busy fishing centre. Pierre D'Aroupet and Jean Hiriat, two French fish merchants, turned the small village of Petit-de-Grat into a major port. Earlier in the century, Acadians enticed to Île Royale by France found much more prosperity in the cod fishery than in trying to farm the island's famously poor soil, and they moved to the island in large numbers. It's likely Josette encountered many of these island residents whenever they came to the mainland to trade or for family events. Perhaps it was from these interactions that she gleaned the idea to head for the island with her family to escape the British.

Josette remembered well the stories she had heard three years ago from kin fleeing the deportations on the mainland. The British would burn everything they found to stop escapees of the raiding parties from returning to their homes. But Josette and her family had a long journey ahead of them, and they knew they had to leave almost all their possessions behind. It could be months or even years before they could safely resettle. Josette likely knew she'd never again see the home where she and her husband had spent nearly a decade raising their children in their self-imposed exile. But by now she was used to life on the run, and at least it was late summer. The woods were dry; the air was pleasant. She had faith they'd find somewhere to call home before winter came.

Like most others who fled into the woods during the autumn of 1758, Josette probably headed to the local Mi'kmaq for help because they knew the geography, how to use the land to survive, and how to keep a safe distance from the raiding parties. According to Mi'kmaw scholars like Daniel N. Paul and Sherry Pictou, many Mi'kmaq by now identified the British as their enemy, too, and they took in Acadian refugees and cared for them as their own. Long histories between the two groups helped the amicable relationship take root, but the threat of British domination solidified the bond. Especially in Île Royale, the Acadians and the Mi'kmaq had become partners and, through marriage, often family as well. The children born of such unions were accepted equally in both cultures.

Those who did find refuge with the Mi'kmaq were the lucky ones. Amherst's soldiers did not hang around Louisbourg long to celebrate. Just weeks after the fortress fell, they scattered across Île Royale in search of Acadians who had yet to flee their lands. Similarly, Andrew Rollo wasted no time preparing his ships for Île Saint-Jean. By the middle of August, he set sail with five transports and a schooner. They headed south before making a straight sail to the island. Following the rough coast of Île Royale, the fleet passed several seaside communities. Jeffrey Amherst's patrols would soon land on these same shores and begin filling their holds with families like Josette's.

Josette and her extended clan made for north of the river and then hurried toward the coast. Dotted with saltwater lakes and thick with bogs, the long isolated stretch of coastline on this side of the island acted as the perfect hideout. From the trees, they watched as day after day the ships anchored beyond the crashing waves sent small vessels ashore. And day after day the same small boats returned to the floating prisons, loaded with unlucky souls. No one found Josette and her family. But winter was coming. What would happen to them? What had happened to the family she'd left behind?

CHAPTER EIGHT

Marguerite

Gabriel Rousseau de Villejouin knew the British were coming, and when they did, he quickly surrendered. Louisbourg had fallen, and his tiny garrison on Île Saint-Jean had no hope of resisting Andrew Rollo's assault. He expected the British had come with orders to relieve him of his command of the island, and that he and his small garrison of soldiers at Port-la-Joye would return to France, as Drucourt had after surrendering Louisbourg. Instead, when Rollo and his fleet arrived, Villejouin was astonished to learn that the British intended to completely empty the island of every French-speaking inhabitant. Jeffrey Amherst had grossly underestimated that five hundred Acadians lived on Île Saint-Jean. According to the bishop of Québec's estimate, as many as six thousand people called the island home, and soon after Rollo's fleet dropped anchor, he realized that he would need many more ships.

By August 26, less than a week after Rollo arrived, ships containing seven hundred Acadians were bound for France via a brief stop in Louisbourg. The rest waited for their turn under the watchful eyes of approximately five hundred infantry and rangers assigned to the island to raid, capture, and guard. In October, the extra ships Rollo had ordered from Louisbourg arrived, and soon the remaining prisoners were on their way to cross the Atlantic. Rollo's ships were bigger than the ones Lawrence had rented for the deportations from Nova Scotia three years earlier, but they were by no means vessels of comfort. More than two thousand prisoners were put on-board the sixteen ships that called on Port-la-Joye that fall. Among the deportees were Marguerite Hébert, née LeBlanc, and her family. Like her brother Joseph, Marguerite and her husband had chosen Île Saint-Jean because they believed a French colony would offer them safety that Grand Pré could not. Charles was a long sawyer, and he found plenty of work building houses and farm buildings for the island's burgeoning population of Acadian refugees. Marguerite didn't know where the members of her family who'd remained in Grand Pré had gone, but she knew that the British had reduced her former home to ash. Her youngest son, Jean Pierre, wasn't even a year old when they left. He'd never get to see his birthplace. None of them would see Grand Pré again. But here on Île Saint-Jean, surely they were safe. Marguerite didn't believe the British would take them off French land until the moment it happened.

At least she, Charles, and their three youngest sons were boarded on the same ship. All of them were bound for France, destined for repatriation to a homeland none of them had ever seen, and where they had neither friends nor family. Putting their sails to the wind before the end of October, the convoy squeezed through the mouth of Port-la-Joye Harbour (now known as Charlottetown Harbour) and sailed east toward the narrow channel between mainland Nova Scotia and Île Royale.

Nearly two miles at its widest and just one at the neck, the Strait of Canso is a deadly place in a squall. Sharp rocky ledges line the shore like fangs, quick to snag ships that stray too close. On November 6, 1758, a day after the convoy entered the strait, a fierce wind crossed the water and scattered the fleet. The *Tamerlane* was blown ashore and nearly lost. The next morning, a squall flung the *Parnassus* against the rocks, severely damaging the vessel. Those aboard the two at-risk ships were transferred to the other vessels, further cramming tight quarters. Two ships down, the convoy faced light winds for five days before tragedy struck again. Just as they slid into Chedabucto Bay on the Atlantic side of the passage, the *Richard and Mary* struck a submerged rock, splintering its thick hull boards. The ship listed hard as the captain angled it toward Île Madame. The *Hind* and two other ships turned north to seek assistance at Louisbourg. The *Richard and Mary* sank, but only after everyone on board had the chance to escape. The holds on the remaining ships grew still more crowded. When the fierce weather abated a small party of crew returned to the *Tamerlane* and successfully refloated it. The convoy braced to cross the cold black ocean.

It was late November by the time favourable winds finally blew the fleet east. Leading the *Ruby, Neptune, John and Samuel, Mathias, Patience, Restoration, Supply, Tamerlane, Violet,* and the *Yarmouth* was a ten-gun, four-hundred-tonne ship named *Duke William,* captained by William Nichols. The experienced captain kept a log of the journey, which was subsequently published. This log and Nichols's letters document the convoy's winter crossing, at least from the perspective of those fortunate enough to travel above the holds. Unfortunately, the original has not survived, but writer George Winslow Barrington drew from Nichols's records and cross-referenced those with other, more fragmentary accounts to reconstruct the voyage. He published an abridged version of the original journal in 1880 as part of a volume titled *Remarkable Voyages and Shipwrecks.*

Barrington's account puts the ships three days off Canso when they faced a terrible squall. The air was thick with sleet, and the waves turned into mountains of water. The *Duke*, large and capable, carried itself over the waves with ease and stuck to its course. But the high waves of the storm made it impossible for the fleet to stay together or keep in view. When the storm finally passed, those in the holds unfamiliar with the open ocean in winter, like Marguerite and Charles, might well have thought the worst was over. Nichols took advantage of the calm sea to look for the sails of the other ships but could see nothing on the horizon. And many more storms were coming, storms fiercer than the one they had just endured.

On December 10, even as another storm began to rage, Nichols spotted a sail in the far distance. When the *Duke* caught up to it, he found the *Violet* in a terrible state. Its hull was filling with water faster than the crew could pump it out, and the captain feared his ship would sink within hours. Locked in its holds were close to four hundred Acadian prisoners. Nichols tried to reef the sail and stay with the ship, but the strong gale that had been slowly picking up made that impossible. He knew the only way to be of any help to the ailing vessel was to stay close to it until the weather cleared and his crew could attempt a rescue.

Nichols retired to his cabin. He filled his pipe with tobacco and sat in a chair to smoke and ponder his options. Suddenly, the floor dropped beneath him, and he was tossed across his cabin. He crashed painfully to the floor. A terrible wave had struck the *Duke*, but the ship was intact. Nichols, exhausted, threw himself across his bed and closed his eyes. Before he could find sleep, a hard knock rattled his cabin door. A member of his crew reported that water had submerged the keelson (the centreline beam of the ship that connects the floor members to the keel), and was rising fast. The ship was leaking, and the storm continued to pound the hull.

Water rushed in fast through the shattered wood. Nichols called on the prisoners to pump. They pumped all night, and when the sun finally rose over a becalmed ocean, the morning rays exposed a terrible sight. While those aboard the *Duke* had fought for their lives and managed to keep the rising water at bay, those on the *Violet* weren't so lucky. It lay turned over on its broadside, the masts splintered, sails swamped, and the crew in obvious distress. A sudden, violent squall struck, and the prisoners continued to labour over the *Duke*'s pumps. When the weather cleared once more, the *Violet* had vanished below the waves, taking twenty-six crew members and its entire load of prisoners. Where the rest of the transport had gone was anyone's guess. The *Duke* was, apparently, floundering alone on the vast Atlantic.

That ship wasn't, however, alone in its distress. After the *Ruby* and its 310 prisoners were separated from the rest of the convoy in the first storm, the vessel developed a serious leak that threatened to completely submerge it. Knowing they were near the Azores, a cluster of lush volcanic islands roughly eleven hundred nautical miles from the entrance to the Mediterranean Sea, the *Ruby*'s captain, William Kelly, headed toward Faial Island, in desperate hope to make land. Instead, strong winds forced the *Ruby* past Faial and straight into the rocks of Pico, a large island to the east of Faial and home to the towering peak of Mount Pico, a 2,300-metre stratovolcano. In the shadow of the ominous mountain, the *Ruby's* hull splintered and buckled, tossing crew and prisoners alike into the cool and churning water. The rocks quickly tore the *Ruby* to pieces, and it disappeared beneath the foamy white surface. Those able to swim struggled in the high seas. Some were able to make it to shore. Those who couldn't swim sank faster than the carcass of the broken vessel. Of the Acadians on board, 190—more than half of its complement—drowned. William Street, the British government's representative in the Azores, noted in a letter to London that "One Hundred & Twenty French & Twenty Three English People were saved." Street further noted that he had arranged for the survivors' passage to Portsmouth on the *Sta Catherina,* a Portuguese schooner.

The *Sta Catherina* sailed into Portsmouth Harbour in early February 1759, "having on-board 87 Prisoners from St. Johns who were cast away in the Ruby Transport there." What happened to the other thirty-three Acadian survivors can only be assumed. They may have succumbed to disease, or perhaps they slipped away from their charges and masqueraded as French sailors. Regardless of their fate, they likely fared better than their friends and family aboard the *Duke.*

Oblivious to the *Ruby's* fate and with its own hull still leaking badly, the *Duke William* pushed on toward Europe. Knowing their situation was dire, Nichols distributed what was left of their rations of food and liquor. The crew lashed empty wine casks and beer barrels to the deck sides to add buoyancy. The priest Jacques Girard of the parish of Pointe-Prime, one of the larger communities on Île Saint-Jean before the Expulsion, tended the spiritual needs of the ill-fated prisoners as death loomed. Nichols surmised that his ship must be nearing Land's End at the western tip of England. For three days, they bailed and drank and prayed, hoping every second to hear the ship's lookout announce that he'd sighted land. Were it not for a thick fog, a faint outline of England's shore may have shown itself and inspired the weary crew and prisoners to double their efforts, but it remained hidden. Nichols knew the ship had little time left and consulted with an elderly prisoner, whom he coined "the father of all of St. Jean's." He thanked the old man for his people's help but told him that it was all for naught. The ship was doomed, and so were they. They had only two small craft capable of removing people from the ship: a longboat and a small cutter. The high waters and hard wind would make it nearly impossible to launch either one. Everyone needed to prepare for death. The crew and their captain would go down with them, Nichols said, as duty dictated.

Historians believe the Acadian elder was Noel Doiron. He had fled the Cobeguit area for Île Saint-Jean before the Expulsion began in 1755. According to Nichols's account, Doiron told the captain that the Acadians accepted their fate and saw no reason why the crew shouldn't save themselves if they could. As the waves began to swamp the deck, Nichols ordered his crew to cut the lines holding the cutter and longboat and prepare to abandon ship. He invited Father Girard to join him, and they stepped over the rails. Together they and the crew rowed away from the doomed ship, consigning the prisoners to a watery grave. Nearly 360 Acadians died on the *Duke William*.

Many long hours passed before the fog lifted and those on the cutter and longboat saw the unmistakable silhouette of St. Michael's Mount, near England's extreme southwest tip. Numb and near death, they landed on a sandy beach and made their way to the nearest light, a tavern, with a harrowing story to tell.

The ships that survived the storms limped across the Atlantic and finally made land near the end of January at the French port of Saint Malo. In the absence of ship manifests, we can't know which ship Marguerite, Charles, and their sons sailed on. Lists of landed deportees were compiled in Saint Malo, however. Five of the transports that left the same day as the *Duke William*, *Ruby*, and *Violet* are grouped together on these lists, and that's where Marguerite and her family finally appear. They were either on the *Yarmouth, Patience, Restoration, John and Samuel*, or the *Mathias*. When they finally made it into port, the five ships were badly battered, and the ranks of the prisoners severely depleted: of the 1,033 who had been put aboard the five ships at Île Saint-Jean, nearly half had died during the crossing.

How they died is unknown. The ways that one can perish at sea are many, each one as terrible as the last. Among the dead listed on the five ships that arrived in Saint Malo in January 1759 is Jean Pierre, Marguerite and Charles's youngest child. He was five years old. Their oldest son, also named Charles, Joseph, aged ten, and another son, walked off the ship the day it landed to find themselves in a strange new place, without money, a dwelling, or Marguerite. She may have fallen overboard at sea. Perhaps a stray yardarm crushed her skull during a rare visit above deck. Or maybe sadness turned her against herself during the darkest days of the voyage, trapped in the dank hold, cradling in her arms the corpse of her youngest son.

Most likely though, she died of disease. Parasites, viruses, and bacteria thrived aboard ships, growing and multiplying in poorly stored food, contaminated drinking water, and in the festering swamps of bilge water in the ship's bottom-most compartment. Maybe she fell victim to scurvy, an often fatal vitamin C deficiency that causes the gums to rot, teeth to fall out, blood to pour from the face, purpling skin, mental detachment, and finally death. During the Seven Years War, the British Navy lost tens of thousands of sailors to this scourge of the sea. Or perhaps it was typhus, a bacterial infection spread by body lice, mites, and fleas, causing high fevers, painful rashes, delirium, and death. Typhus ravaged European armies, killing millions. Typhoid fever could also have been responsible for her early death. The deadly bacteria causes high fevers, sharp abdominal pains, and brain damage. Some sufferers of typhoid slip into coma vigils, unconscious states where the infected person's eyes remain open but their brain stops responding. Her cause of death also could have been dysentery acquired from bad drinking water. The water on oceanic crossings was rarely clean, especially that given to prisoners. Coming in many forms, dysentery reduced a person to violent and constant bouts of diarrhea that caused severe and often fatal dehydration. Or maybe her lungs filled with fluid, slowly choking her to death among the crowded, dank, infectious atmosphere of the ship's lower decks. Preying on the young, old, or weak, pneumonia was particularly deadly for the prisoners in poorly ventilated quarters. However it happened, Marguerite died among her family.

Despite the number of ways to die en route, not only her husband and dependent sons lived, but so did two of her grown daughters, Anne and Isabelle. They had travelled on a different ship and were mercifully spared having to witness their mother's and brother's deaths. There was no welcoming party for the grief-stricken and exhausted prisoners when they arrived in Saint Malo. France was not their home. They shared a language and a distant history, but this was a strange land. Marguerite's great-grandfather, Daniel LeBlanc, was born in France, a little over three hundred miles south in the Poitou region, but he left when he was young. Others had a similarly distant connection; none thought of France as homeland. With what little they had left, Charles and his brood wandered into the walled city to start a new life, having no idea of what life on the continent would hold for them in just a few short years.

CHAPTER NINE

Cécile

The scrawl of a goose-feather quill on a mid-winter day in Paris marked the end of the Seven Years War. The British had conquered Québec in 1759 and Montréal in 1760. New France was no more. Hundreds of thousands had died on the battlefields of Europe as long-held borders inched back and forth. Finally, in February 1763, both sides gathered in Paris to negotiate the terms of peace.

France lost all of its colonies in North America, with the exception of two small islands off the coast of Newfoundland, Saint-Pierre and Miquelon. Retaining those gave French fishermen a place to provision their ships and dry their catches of cod. France also kept the Caribbean island of Guadeloupe, an important source of sugar, and reacquired its former possessions on the Indian subcontinent. Spain took possession of the lands west of the Mississippi River. The British received much of New France, including the colony of Canada (the modern-day province of Quebec), territory east of the Mississippi, and the remnants of Acadia (Acadie Francaise, Île Saint-Jean, and Île Royale). The British no longer feared a violent uprising by the French-speakers. Instead of deporting the people of the newly created province of Quebec, the British allowed them to remain on their lands, practise their Catholic faith, and speak French, but they lived under British law and were banned from holding public office. They were, in short, second-class citizens, but they fared much better than the many Indigenous Peoples who also called the newly British land home. They were not consulted in the redistribution of land or political alignment, not even the Nations that had fought with the British, nor were their land claims recognized or provided for.

For the Acadians clinging to life in the British colonies, the end of the war provided them the freedom to move, but where would they go? Their ancestral lands had been given to Protestant settlers, and even if they went to Quebec, what would they do? The British class system afforded them few opportunities to carve out much of a life. Wherever they went, they would be disadvantaged. At least they were still in North America. For their friends and family in England and France, the end of the war simply meant the beginning of a new stage of exile.

Cécile Landry, née LeBlanc, could taste the rich and salty air, thick against her dry lips. It reminded her of home. The outgoing tide that had brought her on the ship *L'Ambition* had left a rye-yellow seafloor draped in tangled seaweed and ocean debris. The tides around Saint Malo were almost as dramatic as those in the Bay of Fundy. At high tide, Saint Malo was an island fortress; at low tide, it was surrounded by sand.

Connected to the mainland by a narrow, ancient causeway, the city was heavily fortified and for good reason: Saint Malo was a city of pirates. Endowed with a royal decree to ply the nation's coasts and commandeer any enemy vessel they came across, the privateer legions of Brittany, known as corsairs, quickly became famous for their skill at high-seas conquest. The corsairs plundered thousands of English merchant ships in the sixteenth and seventeenth centuries. Between a quarter and third of their takings went to the French Crown. Saint Malo's armed batteries, thick walls, and castles made it a haven for the corsairs. The city's leaders fought bitterly with French and Breton authorities over freedom and independence, insisting that the fortified outpost was autonomous. The towering medieval ramparts and bustling cobbled streets of Saint Malo were a stark contrast to the pastoral communities the Acadians had known.

Cécile shuffled through the narrow city streets among a mob of exiles, curious onlookers, and French officials. The Gothic cathedral of Saint Malo, the religious centre of the city since the twelfth century, loomed ever-present in her peripheral vision. Seagulls screamed in the sky, filling out a chorus of port city sounds, clunking tackles, and barked orders in the languages of the sea: Breton, French, Gallo, Spanish, Portuguese.

The pirate city wasn't the first Old World port Cécile had laid eyes on from the decks of a sailing ship. Like her brother Jean Baptiste, Cécile and her husband, Charles Landry, had spent most of the last eight years locked up in a dockside prison in Southampton, England. At least she hadn't been on her own. In addition to her brother and her husband, her daughters were with her, too: Marguerite, twenty-two; Marie Madeleine, seventeen; Genevieve, fifteen; and Marie-Josèphe, thirteen. Somehow, against the odds, they had all survived the deportation to Virginia, the harsh winter in the boats, the terrible crossing of the Atlantic, and the long stay in the

Southampton prison camp. If they were still in Acadia, her oldest daughters would be married by now, raising families of their own. But they weren't.

In 1763, French ships brought Cécile, her family, and approximately 750 other Acadians to Brittany from their English prisons. It wasn't a selfless act of altruism on the part of the French. Rather, France saw the exiles as the solution to a problem. France's population was in decline, and the Acadian fecundity was nearly legendary. Acadia's population had grown from just a handful of original families to thousands of people. Sieur de Dièreville, a botanist and poet, had spent a year in Acadia in 1700 and eight years later published his observations. He found families with fifteen to twenty living children. After talking to the locals and discovering how common this was, he wrote that Acadians seemed to have a "capacity in the business" of rearing children.

The Duke of Nivernois, Louis-Jules Barbon Mancini-Mazarini, a French aristocrat of Italian ancestry, proposed that France remove the nearly 800 Acadians imprisoned in England, the equivalent of 120 families, and settle them in France. As France's ambassador to England, Nivernois was familiar with the conditions in which the Acadians languished. He requested that Louis XV provide 120,000 livres to settle the families in France. This was a hefty sum, the equivalent of nearly $21 million in today's currency, but Nivernois was confident the venture would prove profitable within two years. The king agreed, and Cécile and the rest of the prisoners in England sailed for France.

Fellow Acadians did not flood the streets to greet their newly arrived kin. Few, if any actually lived within the city walls. Saint Malo itself contained few residences. These were found onshore, adjacent to the island, on the sandy marshland flanking the mouth of the Rance River. This is where the Acadians lived, who had survived the long crossing from Île Saint-Jean in 1758. Like her predecessors, Cécile was given six sols a day, barely enough to buy bread and butter, let alone feed, clothe, and house a family of six and a far cry from what she and her husband possessed before the Expulsion. According to an assessment of their possessions recorded in 1755, they owned a large plot of land, six buildings, seven cows, fifty-two sheep, twenty hogs, and two horses.

Cécile settled into her new life. She had no other choice. Her brother lived close, and when they arrived in Saint Malo, they learned that although their sister Marguerite had perished, her husband and two of her sons were nearby. But if the Acadians had sailed to France believing that they would be given land to farm, they were mistaken. France's foreign minister at the time, Étienne-François duc de Choiseul, was the man in charge of the exiles' daily allowance. Anxious to transform the exiles from dependents to contributors, Choiseul (and many other leading French political strategists and economists) thought the future of the kingdom's success lay in the tropics. Nivernois had convinced Choiseul of what he perceived as the Acadians' "tenacious attachment for France" and "tireless" work ethic. Choiseul saw the Acadians as the perfect people to send to French Guiana on the northeast coast of South America. The colony was largely considered a failure since it was originally settled in the early decades of the seventeenth century. Thanks to tropical diseases, colonial mismanagement, and neglect, the mortality rate of French Guiana's early settlers approached a staggering 84 per cent. France's slave-dependent, sugar-producing colonies in the Caribbean needed regular provisioning and constant military assistance, as the English, Portuguese, and Dutch—also keen to bolster and grow their own sugar and slave industries in the region—threatened France's presence.

For decades, the French had tried to attract white settlers to these colonies, but they failed because Europeans feared what would happen if the slaves who outnumbered them were to revolt. Guiana's vast unmapped interior provided escaped slaves with the ideal place to hide. The French called the hidden jungle villages they established "maroon camps." Choiseul was convinced that a strong population of white settlers at Guiana would represent French power and support France's sugar trade. But when he shared his plan with the Acadians, few accepted, even when Choiseul threatened to cancel their meagre allowance. It apparently had not occurred to Choiseul that after everything the exiles had endured, they would find the prospect of yet another upheaval, yet another long journey, yet another new beginning in a strange land completely abhorrent. The Acadians had the power to choose their fate now, and the greater number of them refused the tropical option. They also mostly rejected proposals to send them to Haiti or the Îles Malouines (now the Falkland Islands).

Against the odds, however, some accepted and once again took to the sea in search of a new life. Their hopes were dashed quickly and horridly. Nearly all those who did leave France that year faced great difficulties. Tropical diseases decimated the Kourou settlement in Guiana. Some of the families who survived the first few months remained, but many others left, either to try their luck in the Caribbean or to return to France.

The group of Acadians that braved the harsh southern conditions of the Îles Malouines managed relatively well, but in 1767 France signed the colony over to Spain, and most of the existing settlers were forced to return to France. The Acadians, like Cécile and her family, who chose to stay in France were aware of their value, and they began to negotiate for better terms. Some hoped to establish a new Acadia within France itself. Millions of acres of French farmland lay fallow, mostly because noble landowners had chosen not to have their land worked. The Acadians' ingenuity, determination, and hard work had transformed the Maritime wilderness into rich agricultural land, and the French recognized the economic benefits the Acadians offered.

Off the west coast of Brittany lay Belle-Île-en-Mer. For centuries, the island was the neglected possession of the absent noble families that owned its land. In 1761, the British attacked and nearly destroyed Belle-Île-en-Mer. Approximately nine thousand British soldiers landed on the island, laid siege to the castle at Le Palais, wiped out the livestock, and decimated almost every square inch of arable land. When the French surrendered, the British ripped down every wood structure still standing and used the lumber for firewood and to repair their ships. Once the war was over, the people of Belle-Île-en-Mer, the Bellilois, needed help.

Three Acadians living in Morlaix, a city roughly ninety-three miles west of Saint Malo, travelled to the island to assess the soil and conditions. That they regarded the war-ravaged island, peopled with the Breton-speaking Bellilois, as a place where their exiled brethren could rebuild their lives says a great deal about the Acadians' determination to choose their own fate. They estimated that, under the right conditions, nearly eighty families could comfortably settle on the island. In exchange, they told Choiseul, they would require their own parish; they would not be subject to the rule of others. They also asked for masons to come from the mainland and teach them stone building techniques. They wanted their six sol allowance extended and an exemption from taxes while they established the new community. Choiseul agreed to send stonemasons, to continue the allowance until their first harvest, and to exempt them from taxes. But he balked at the request for an autonomous parish. He wanted the hard-working Acadians to influence the Bellilois, whom the island's governor, Baron de Warren, deemed "very lazy, and who possess no industry." The Acadians accepted these terms and in the autumn of 1765 prepared to leave the mainland.

Cécile's brother Jean Baptiste and the woman he had married in England had young children of their own by now, and decided to move to Belle-Île-en-Mer. It was here, two years later in 1767, that Jean Baptiste would sit down and make the declaration of his ancestry. Cécile and Charles had reservations about the move. They knew that the British had attacked and seized the island in the past. What would stop them from trying again? Would the Acadians move there only to be expelled by the colonizing English all over again? And what about the farming conditions? Were they to rely on the good word of the compatriots from Morlaix who claimed the soil was fertile and ready to be worked? Belle-Île-en-Mer was no paradise, regardless of what the French government or motivated Acadians might say. Cécile and Charles decided to stay put.

Abbé Le Loutre joined the eighty or so families who signed on to the Belle-Île-en-Mer plan as their priest. He had fled to Quebec during the Expulsion and was sailing for France when the British captured his ship. They imprisoned him on the island of Jersey for the remainder of the war. Once freed, he returned to Brittany, his birthplace, and began advocating for Acadian rights in France. The Acadians on Belle-Île-en-Mer worked hard, but the soil was bad, the livestock was diseased, and the locals were hostile. Within six years, the settlement plan had failed, and most of the families that had tried to make a new home on the rocky island returned to the mainland.

Those who were not tempted by the fields of Belle-Île-en-Mer or the far-flung exotic locales made do in the shanty towns on the fringe of whatever port city they happened to land in when they arrived in France. The six sols per day they received were enough to feed and clothe them, but the allowance still placed them among the poorest of the working French, the day labourers and servants. Landless and barely surviving, the Acadians slipped into the inequitable economic fabric of French culture at the time. While a very few enjoyed the lavish lifestyles commonly associated with the French nobility—decadent chateaus, ornate dress, and lascivious hedonism—most in France clung to life amidst the squalor of poverty. Food shortages were common, and most ate little more than rough rye bread, buckwheat porridge, and soup each day. Even the abundant wine France had long been known for was out of reach, particularly in Brittany and Normandy. Feet were clad with rough-hewn wooden shoes cleated with nails, and clothes were carved from sheets of canvas. Disease commonly ripped through rural poor communities, killing eighty thousand in Brittany alone in 1741. Death loomed everywhere. Petty theft or counterfeiting carried the brutal punishment of being broken on the wheel. Those accused of heresy, sodomy, and witchcraft were burned at the stake. Those guilty of treason were dismembered, by sword or beast. A paltry allowance kept the impoverished one step from the bottom, but even that was tenuous.

France's economy was near ruin: the long war had drained France's coffers, a series of postwar tax hikes had failed to produce needed revenue, and political and public support for accommodating the refugees had all but waned. During Louis XV's reign, he had lost vast swathes of territory, several conflicts, and even the confidence of the nobility. Less than two years before the first group of Acadians arrived on French shores, the king was very nearly assassinated when Robert-François Damiens pushed through a line of guards and stabbed the king in the side. (For his crime he was drawn and quartered and then burned on a large bonfire. His family was banished from France, and his house was burned to the ground.) The king remained open to schemes to put the Acadian refugees to use and relieve the state of the burden. It was an auspicious time for one Louis-Nicolas, Marquis de Pérusse des Cars to step forward with a proposal.

Wounded during the Seven Years War at the Battle of Kloster Kamp — a large battle in western Germany near the present-day border with the Netherlands — Pérusse retired to recover at a large chateau in the Poitou region, given to him as part of his wife's dowry. When the marquis arrived to nurse his battle wounds, he was shocked at what he found. Endless plots of arable land lay fallow and unused, a situation common throughout

France that was the product of aristocratic malfeasance and neglect. He vowed to transform his thousands of acres into productive farmland, an ambition that would require hundreds of agricultural labourers.

Poitou was a land that time had forgotten, still worked by hand as it had been centuries prior. The French government realized that the low-lying fields of Poitou, marked with shallow rivers, ancient forests, and fertile marshlands, were an ideal place to put the Acadians to work. Henri Bertin, the king's adviser on agricultural matters, presented to Pérusse the idea of having the Acadians work the marquis's fields. Pérusse signed on immediately. The Acadians seemed the ideal workforce, and Pérusse calculated that if he could recruit a small group to work for him, the rest would follow. He pledged to build small villages across his estate where they could thrive — a new Acadia.

Word of the scheme spread quickly through the Acadian communities in Brittany. Posters went up. The priests spoke about it at Mass, where Cécile and Charles probably heard about it. The proposal seemed perfect: vast fields of open farmland, large stone and wood farmhouses, and the chance to establish tightly knit communities far from the grasp of the British. They prepared to leave.

When Cécile and her family moved to Poitou, she was fifty-seven years old, and she had been an exile for nearly twenty years, over a third of her life. They left Saint Malo and sailed to La Rochelle. From there, they travelled overland, by wagon, to the town of Châtellerault. They arrived in the middle of October. The trees were just starting to turn. Lazy heat still drifted across the fields. They were among the first to arrive of the nearly fifteen hundred Acadians who had agreed to Pérusse's proposal.

Incredibly, they arrived to find yet another disappointment awaiting them. The marquis had built only a handful of the houses he had promised. They had travelled a considerable distance to find themselves homeless yet again. Pérusse arranged with various people in Châtellerault to board the Acadians while the builders got to work. Sadly, neither Cécile nor Charles would live to see the new Acadia. During their first spring in Poitou, both died. They were buried in the graveyard at Châtellerault, far from the red clay banks of the Bay of Fundy.

CHAPTER TEN

Survival

Cécile and Charles's daughter Genevieve Landry was only seven years old when she was sent into exile. She grew up moving from place to place, first to Virginia, then to England, then to Brittany, and finally to Poitou. She was twenty-six when both her parents passed away, shortly after they moved their family to what was promised as a new Acadia. At least she had somewhere to live, and at first things seemed as though they were improving. Within a few short years, though, the Poitou settlement failed.

Louis XV died the same year as Genevieve's parents, and in the wake of his death, France experienced radical change. Anne Robert Jacques Turgot, formerly the tax collector for the region of Limoges, was promoted to controller-general of finance and was determined to save France's economy. Pérusse's settlement in Poitou, costing the Crown nearly six hundred thousand livres a year, was seen as an expensive royal favour. It was the first item on Turgot's chopping block. He demanded that half the Acadians at Poitou remove themselves from the settlement and head to either Corsica or Île de France in the Indian Ocean (now Mauritius). If neither of those options appealed to them, the government would pay for their transportation to the port city of Nantes, where they would resume living on the small allowance that had supported them when they first arrived in France.

In retrospect, Turgot's plan seems counterproductive, perhaps even a deliberate attempt to destroy Pérusse's settlement. Turgot wanted to push the Acadians to Nantes because he could more easily ship them off to one of France's tropical colonies or, perhaps, back to North America. Pérusse, though angered by the move, had little power to stop it. Many of the Acadian families who had relocated to Poitou had already discovered that the soil was much poorer than they'd been promised. Of the choices that Turgot endeavoured to tempt them with, they opted to move to Nantes. Genevieve was among them.

Perhaps rumours of a new life for Acadians back in North America helped to sway them. Family and friends in British North America were sending word across the Atlantic that a new refuge had been found in the postwar landscape. It seemed like a paradise. Genevieve and the rest of her generation were tired of being pawns in France's crumbling political system. If the news coming from North America could be believed, they needed to get themselves to a port city and out of France. Lucky for them, the king of Spain had a vast piece of land he was eager to populate with new settlers.

Genevieve made her way to Nantes at an ideal time. In 1783, a smooth-talking businessman by the name of Henri Peyroux de la Coudreniere had arrived in the city after spending the previous seven years in Louisiana, which then stretched over most of the North American plains: from the Great Lakes in the north to the Gulf of Mexico in the south and from the western borders of Georgia and Florida in the east, to the Spanish lands of Mexico (now Texas) in the west. Peyroux had returned to France with a grand scheme he believed would make him a small fortune. First, he knew of the unhappy Acadian population scattered through British North America and France, and second, he knew that Spain had acquired Louisiana from the French at the end of the Seven Years War, and was anxious to boost the colony's population. At the time, Louisiana was mostly inhabited by French settlers from France and Canada and thousands of African slaves, the result of France's participation in the slave trade. Peyroux, working on behalf of the Spanish Crown, saw the Acadians as the perfect answer to both issues. Counting on Spain's desire to resist British dominance in the region, he correctly assumed that Spain would offer abundant land, pay for the transportation costs for the exiles he would recruit from France, and reward him handsomely for solving its immigration problem.

Peyroux arrived in Nantes ready to promote his scheme, but he needed a trusted Acadian figure from the community to help him. While visiting an Acadian cobbler to get his shoes fixed, he met the man he was looking for: Olivier Terrio. Originally from Grand Pré, like Genevieve, he was a small child when the British deported him and his family. Now in his thirties, he dreamed of a better life, but he saw no way to improve his situation in France. When Peyroux told him of his plan, Terrio was enthusiastic enough to brave the skepticism of those Acadians who were justifiably and thoroughly disenchanted with settlement schemes. By 1783, nearly every Acadian family in France had participated in one or more of the various plans dreamed up in the aftermath of the war: South America, the Caribbean,

Belle-Île-en-Mer, and Poitou. Poor planning, corruption, and greed were primarily to blame for the failures of these schemes. Politicians, estate owners, middlemen, even priests had led them to this settlement or that for their own financial benefit. Not one of them had actually offered the Acadians an opportunity to get back on their feet and thrive. It stood to reason: why should Louisiana be any different?

The older generation of exiles might not have listened to Terrio with enthusiasm, but the people of Genevieve's generation were receptive. The Expulsion and its aftermath had been hardest on their parents. They were the ones who lost everything and had to shoulder the considerable burden of caring and providing for children through years of hardship. Now those children were adults with families of their own. They saw Louisiana as a place where they could put down roots and return to an Acadian way of life on their own land. To his dismay, at first Terrio could convince only four people to commit to the plan, but when the Spanish king agreed to cover the costs of transportation and resettlement, more and more Acadians warmed to the idea of leaving the old world for the new.

By the time the first ships left in the spring of 1785, almost two-thirds of the Acadians living in France, approximately fifteen hundred people, had agreed to join the new settlement. Genevieve was among them. She and 273 other exiles boarded *La Bergère* in early May; Olivier Terrio and his family were part of the group, as was Genevieve's younger sister Marie-Josèphe. The crossing was considerably more comfortable than when Genevieve had travelled from Grand Pré to Virginia, or from Virginia to Southampton. Spain determined its settlers would survive the voyage and so had outfitted the transport ships with plenty of room for the Acadians, their possessions, generous stores of food, water, and firewood, as well as a dedicated doctor for each ship.

On a humid August breeze, after a three-month crossing, *La Bergère* entered the mouth of the Mississippi River. Since they were first forced out of Acadia, Genevieve and Marie-Josèphe had travelled more than nine thousand miles to arrive in a place they could truly call home.

The Acadians who relocated from France to Louisiana in 1785 were not the first to settle in the former French colony. Acadian exiles had arrived in Louisiana nearly twenty years earlier. The British had captured the Acadian leader Joseph Broussard in 1762 and imprisoned him in Halifax for the remainder of the Seven Years War. As soon as he was released, Broussard chartered a ship and led two hundred Acadians from Halifax to the French colony of Saint Domingue (now Haiti), where a few hundred Acadians were already living, constructing a naval base for the French. Neither the climate nor the tropical diseases agreed with Broussard and his followers, and he soon decided to sail up the Mississippi River toward the Illinois country. Broussard arrived in New Orleans in the winter of 1765 and found a colony in transition. Spain had recently acquired Louisiana but had not yet sent anyone to govern the region. The acting French governor welcomed Broussard and the Acadians with open arms and offered them a grant of land west of New Orleans on Bayou Teche.

The marshlands around Bayou Teche suited the Acadians, and they began sending letters to family and friends still stuck in British North America, urging them to come to Louisiana. Marie Marguerite LeBlanc, the oldest daughter of Bénoni, was living in Maryland at the time. With the war over, Maryland wanted the Acadian exiles gone, but long years of deprivation made it impossible for them to cover the costs of any journey. The exiles petitioned the government for a safe return to Nova Scotia, or the province of Quebec where they could rebuild their lives, but the trip was deemed too expensive. Word of the Acadian settlement in Louisiana had reached the Chesapeake Bay area, and Maryland administrators knew that shipping the Acadians there would be cheaper than arranging their transport to Quebec. Nearly every Acadian in the colony jumped at the chance to leave.

The Acadians spread out across three separate communities north and west of New Orleans. Some went farther up the Mississippi, settling outside the town of Baton Rouge. A small group settled in the swamps of the south, near the Gulf Coast. Travelling with her young husband-to-be, Germain Bergeron, in the late 1760s, Marie Marguerite reached New Orleans and settled in St. James parish. She and Germain married on the banks of the Mississippi in 1768. In Louisiana, the Acadians found a stable place to settle for the first time since the Expulsion began. Their land-clearing and water-management skills were well suited to the flat lands of the many river basins and bayous of southern Louisiana. Instead of growing rye and wheat, they grew sugar cane. They were welcome to speak their language and practise their religion.

When Genevieve and Marie-Josèphe arrived in 1785, they found not only Marie Marguerite but also a few other relatives in the new colony. Genevieve and her sister settled on the banks of Bayou Lafourche, among the cypress and tupelo wetlands, in the parish of Assumption, where a large group of Acadians had already settled. More than twenty-five hundred Acadians called Louisiana home, and their contributions to the state's unique culture are unmistakable. Their descendants, known now as Cajuns, live there still at upwards of eight hundred thousand people — the largest population of Acadian descendants in the world.

Other Acadians in Britain's American colonies headed in the opposite direction once the war ended. Madeleine LeBlanc and her family were among those searching for a new home. During the war they lived in Braintree, on the outskirts of Boston. Massachusetts had no intention of paying for the passage of now-free exiles to Louisiana. Madeleine and her family headed for the province of Quebec. Unlike some of their children, François and Jeanne had survived both the Expulsion and all the years of hardship that followed. They, along with hundreds of others, also made the journey north.

Not all the exiles left the colonies after the war. Some remained in the cities and towns they were sent to and assimilated into the local population, anglicizing their names and trying to begin anew. There is no record of when Anne died, but it is likely she remained in Philadelphia until her final hour. Bénoni, too, died in the colonies, most likely in Maryland, before 1763. He would have just entered his thirties. His older brother Jacques, sent to Massachusetts alongside Madeleine, her family, and their parents, passed away before the rest left the colony.

Small traces of the legacy of the Acadians in France can still be found today, most prominently at the former site of the Poitou settlement (near the modern town of Archigny). Several of the farmsteads constructed to house the families brought to the region in 1772 still stand there. Jean Baptiste, after leaving Belle-Île-en-Mer, was one of those who remained. He and his wife both died in France many years after the ships left for Louisiana.

Those who managed to escape the major deportations, especially the families who spent long years hiding in the forests of the Saint John River Valley, went on to the province of Quebec to join their relatives who settled there after the war. Others settled in the Madawaska region of New Brunswick. Among them was Marie's family, who appear in church records across the region, from Québec to Fredericton. Some of her children were among large groups who chose to remain in New Brunswick but clung stubbornly to their own language, culture, and religion. Their determination to survive has made New Brunswick the heartland of modern Acadian culture.

Josette was able to scrape by in the forests of Île Royale until it was safe to come out of hiding. She eventually made it to Île Madame and settled there with many other Acadian families. Able to find work in the lucrative fishing industry on the small island, her descendants live there still, active members of one of the largest Acadian communities in modern Nova Scotia. Joseph's widow, Marie-Josèphe, escaped the deportations of Île Saint-Jean in 1758, and made her way to a refugee camp in northern New Brunswick. She remarried and spent the remaining years of the war on the run, fleeing from one camp to another as the British swept the region on their push to take Québec near the end of the war. With her new husband and many children in tow, she eventually returned to her old home in Havre de la Fortune on Île Saint-Jean, which had become part of Nova Scotia during the negotiation of the Treaty of Paris. She remained on the island for the rest of her days.

When the British later divided the colony from Nova Scotia, named it St. John's Island, and gave it to absentee landowners, Marie-Josèphe and her neighbours became impoverished tenant farmers. The move caused yet another exodus. Marie-Josèphe's youngest son, Georges-Robert (the son still in her womb when her first husband Joseph left the family to return to Acadia) petitioned the colonial council for a land grant along the banks of the Margaree River. The council granted the title, and Georges-Robert joined the small group of Acadians who were moving to the island, what is now Cape Breton, in the 1780s. These families established what would become the largest Acadian community in Nova Scotia, Chéticamp.

Georges-Robert's children remained in the area for several generations before they left for Sydney to work in the burgeoning steel industry. The family finally ended up in Louisbourg, where my great-grandfather Joseph Sylvestre LeBlanc settled and had several children, including my grandfather Robert LeBlanc. Gramp, as I called him, left Louisbourg to fight in Korea in the 1950s. Upon his return home, he was stationed in Mill Cove, a small community on Nova Scotia's South Shore, just ten kilometres up the road from Bayswater, the village I grew up in.

I don't know exactly how the story of the French convict came about or who in my family thought it preferable to claim descent from a French criminal than from hard-working Acadians. But as I worked my way through the family history, it occurred to me that the story wasn't entirely a fantasy. Shipwreck, escape, survival — these are the elements of the Expulsion, at least for my family. The parallels between a French convict caught in a shipwreck during his transportation to a penal colony and the fate of so many of my ancestors are clear. The convict's "adoption" by an Acadian family is echoed in the decades after the Expulsion, when the surviving LeBlancs established new lives and new communities. Perhaps whoever came up with the story of the French convict knew more about the real family history than I thought.

Nearly every physical trace of Acadia had been wiped out or replaced. But no flame, ship, or gun could extinguish the community. Wherever Acadians were sent and remained after the Expulsion, the culture lives on. From a tight-knit group of settlers on the eastern seaboard of the New World come the proud descendants whose dedicated work continues to rebuild our history, our story, and our place in the world.

But our oppressors are slow to release their grip. Acadian communities throughout North America continue to face the lingering effects of post-colonial persecution. Under-representation in government and business has long been an issue in areas with Acadian populations. It wasn't until 1960 that an Acadian was elected as the leader of a province. According to Statistics Canada, unilingual francophones in Nova Scotia and New Brunswick earn nearly $10,000 less per year than their anglophone neighbours. Until recently, francophone school boards were underfunded and regional. Many children in communities outside of more populous francophone areas were left with no educational options in French. My family was not the only one that chose to bury or deny their heritage in search of opportunity and acceptance.

In New Brunswick, the home of the largest Acadian community in Canada, anglophone opponents of the province's
official bilingualism campaign against French, the mother
tongue of nearly 32 per cent of the population. They argue
official bilingualism favours francophones. Yet, according to the
last annual report issued by the Office of the Commissioner
of Official Languages for New Brunswick, francophones make
up two-thirds of the bilingual population of the province, particularly in the public service. Nevertheless, these jobs go not
to francophones but to people who can communicate in both
English and French. Even outside the bilingualism debate, language divides the province, literally, along a diagonal line from
the northwest to the southeast: francophones above the line,
anglophones below. Integration between the two groups is poor.
The hostility that drove Lawrence's Expulsion has not entirely
disappeared from the world yet. The Expulsion was a very visible form of oppression. More subtle discrimination has taken
its place.

The children of Jeanne Hébert and François LeBlanc, spread
as they were around the world to different fates and futures, represent the displacement suffered at large for the entire Acadian
population during the Expulsion. Their stories are, in a sense,
the stories of every person displaced and upended by the actions
of the British government. Even now, all over the world, the political and economic goals of imperial governments result in the
displacement of people every day. The plight of the Rohingya
people in Myanmar in many ways parallels the Expulsion of the
Acadians. A large majority of the Rohingya people live now in
a stateless limbo. Forced from their homes and sent on the run,

they are struggling to survive in vast refugee camps in neighbouring Bangladesh. Their homeland has been razed and
resettled. Religious and ethnic divisions, rooted in the complex
history of the region, keep them from returning to their former
lives. Their expulsion is still very much underway, and it will
define generations of those born into this tragedy. The effects
of the Expulsion on Acadian culture are inseparable from its
modern identity. The same does not have to be true for future
displaced peoples.

ACKNOWLEDGEMENTS

I want to start by thanking my partner, Emily. From listening to me endlessly rant about all things Acadian for years, to helping me through the hardest parts of this long process, your tireless support of me, and this book, was very important to its completion. Thank you. I also want to thank Harry Thurston, who mentored me during the early drafts of this manuscript. Without his initial feedback and support, I would have never tackled this topic. To my parents, Ron and Veronica, and my great-aunt Margie, thank you for helping me discover the first genealogical breadcrumbs that allowed me to approach Stephen A. White with the basic information he needed to plug our family into the general line. Without the detailed and dedicated work of those before me who scoured through hundreds of records, registries, and other primary resources, and reconstructed the family histories of hundreds of thousands of people like me, this book wouldn't have been possible. Finally, thank you to everyone who worked on this book during the publishing process. Special thanks to my wonderful editors, Jill Ainsley and Paula Sarson.

NOTES ON SOURCES

In the words of Erik Larson, author of such bestselling historical non-fictions as *Dead Wake, The Devil in the White City,* and *Isaac's Storm*: "It is one thing to write Great Man history, quite another to explore the lives of history's little men." The most prominent figures associated with the Expulsion of the Acadians left journals, memos, letters, and diaries. The characters in this book did not. The lives of the "great" men of this tragedy have been dissected, retraced, and published in detail by historians analyzing the Seven Years War and its far-reaching global effects (including the Expulsion) on shaping the modern political landscape of North America and the Western world in general. The lives of those torn from their homes, left to die, murdered, or otherwise scattered to the wind have not had as much time in history's limelight. I have relied heavily on primary sources found in the Nova Scotia Archives and on the scholarship of prominent historians who have attempted to present the Expulsion in an unbiased but honest light.

The Contexts of Acadian History, 1686-1784 (1992); *The Acadians: Creation of a People* (1973); and *From Migrant to Acadian* (2004), all by historian Naomi E.S. Griffiths, are must-read books for anyone looking to venture into the world of Acadian history. Griffiths is the pre-eminent scholar on the subject. I also found several of her articles and lecture transcripts incredibly useful in answering the questions of who and what the Acadians were *before* the Expulsion.

I found a wealth of knowledge in Dean Jobb's *The Acadians: A People's Story of Exile and Triumph* (2005), an exhaustively researched and compassionate book. John Mack Faragher's *A Great and Noble Scheme: The Tragic Story of the Expulsion of the French Acadians from Their American Homeland* (2005), though written from an American perspective, also served as a great reference and resource. The same can be said for Christopher Hodson's *The Acadian Diaspora: An Eighteenth-Century History* (2012), particularly for insights into the many destinations the Acadians were sent to during their years of exile. Albert N. Lafreniere's reproduction of Don Landry's *The Acadian Deportation Ships* (1993), published in the French-Canadian Genealogical Society of Connecticut's journal *Connecticut Maple Leaf*, was pivotal in helping to figure out who was on what ship and where they were headed.

Without a doubt, however, the most invaluable resources were the genealogical work done by many Acadian historians, most notably Stephen A. White of the Université de Moncton. White, a LeBlanc descendant himself, is the world's leading Acadian genealogist and the author of the *Dictionnaire généalogique des familles acadiennes* (1999), the definitive guide to Acadian genealogy. Mr. White is currently in the process of adding to and updating this opus, which will surely reveal valuable insight to the world of Acadian history and genealogy.

Chapter One: Bénoni

To reconstruct the reading of the deportation order in Grand Pré, I relied heavily on the journal of Colonel John Winslow (1755).

This informative and emotional primary source, found in the Nova Scotia Archives, is the most comprehensive resource we have regarding the deportations from Grand Pré. Containing almost daily entries written before, during, and after the reading of the deportation order on September fifth, the journal also holds important communications between Winslow, Captain Murray (the commander at Fort Edward), Charles Lawrence, and many others.

The journal of Jeremiah Bancroft, titled *Jeremiah Bancroft at Fort Beauséjour and Grand-Pré* (2013), edited and annotated by Jonathon Fowler and Earle Lockerby, was published for the first time in book form by Gaspereau Press. This is the only other primary source yet recovered that is written from the first-hand point of view of a witness of the deportation at Grand Pré. Bancroft, a solider from New England who participated in the siege of Beauséjour before being sent to Grand Pré under Winslow's command, corroborates Winslow's version of events and gives some additional details that enrich what we know about this historic tragedy.

To reconstruct Monckton's campaign to clear the Chignecto region of its Acadian population, I relied on Bancroft's journal as well as the *Journal of Abijah Willard, English officer present at the capture of Fort Beauséjour in 1755* (1930), edited by John Clarence Webster and published by the New Brunswick Historical Society. Further background reference for the fall of Beauséjour and Monckton's actions came from John Clarence and Alice de Kessler Lusk Webster's *The Life of Thomas Pichon: The Spy of Beausejour* (1937) and *The Siege of Beausejour in 1755: A Journal of the Attack on Beausejour written by Jacau De Fiedmont, Artillery Officer and Acting Engineer at the Fort* (1936) and from Francis Parkman's *France and England in North America vol. 7: Montcalm and Wolfe* (1885). Parkman's account, it must be noted, though informative, needs to be read with an acknowledgement of his pro-English bias. He believed the Acadians to have forced Lawrence to order the Expulsion.

Chapter Two: Jacques

No survivor's accounts of the deportation voyages of 1755 appear to exist. I found the story told to Reverend Brown in Sara J. Beanlands's master's thesis, "Annotated Edition of Rev. Dr. Andrew Brown's Manuscript: 'Removal of the French inhabitants of Nova Scotia by Lieut. Governor Lawrence & His Majesty's Council in October 1755.'" I felt it incredibly important to attempt to reconstruct the voyages. Due to the lack of credible primary sources, this moment of the Expulsion has often been overlooked in the historiography, typically warranting only a line or two.

Chapter Three: Madeleine

To reconstruct colonial Boston as it looked in 1755, I relied on various engravings and sketches of the cityscape found through the American Antiquarian Society. To give a sense of the reception Madeleine and her fellow exiles faced upon arrival, I looked at letters from concerned citizens published in the *Boston Gazette*.

Much of the information regarding Boston's Puritan history came from Cotton Mather's *Magnalia Christi Americana* (1702) and secondary sources.

The notes of officials sent to inspect the vessels are recorded in the *Journals of the House of Representatives of Massachusetts*, Vol. 32 Part I (1755). We know Madeleine and the rest of her immediate family were moved to Braintree, as they appear there in a 1757 census taken by the selectmen of the town. The petitions of Lawrence Mius, Joseph Michel, and other exiles to the colonial council can be found in the *Massachusetts Archives Collection, 1603-1799, vol. 23: French Neutrals, 1755-1758*.

Chapter Four: Anne

The Acadian experience in Pennsylvania is one of the best documented of any deportation destination, thanks to the well-organized and accessible Pennsylvania State Archives. I was able to see how Governor Morris reacted to the arrival of the exiles, how the assembly sought to deal with them, and read the petitions of Galerne, Griffiths, Tibaudat, and Thibaudeau, as well as documents related to the actions of Anthony Benezet in the *Pennsylvania Archives Eighth Series, Vol.1-8*. Luckily, this correspondence has been preserved and was vital to the creation of this chapter. To reconstruct Philadelphia, I relied again on old sketches and engravings as well as various newspaper clippings from the *Pennsylvania Gazette*. I found information regarding the original Philadelphia pesthouse in the *Journal of the Common Council of the City of Philadelphia* (1836-1920).

Chapter Five: Jean Baptiste

Tracing Jean Baptiste's movements involved digging through archival material located in Virginia, England, and France. *The Official Records of Robert Dinwiddie* (published in manuscript form 1883-1884), made available through Yale University and the Virginia Historical Society, reveal exactly how the colonial government handled the reception of the exiles. Among Dinwiddie's papers, many letters to regional governors and officials in London give context for what drove him to keep the prisoners stranded on the ships all winter and eventually evict them to England.

Jean Baptiste's arrival in England, as well as the situation he and the rest of the exiles faced upon landing, is well documented in the Records of the Admiralty, Naval Forces, Royal Marines, Coastguard, and related bodies, found at the National Archives in England.

To help fill out the exiles' experiences once they landed, I also relied on newspaper articles from the time, most importantly *Felix Farley's Bristol Journal* (1820) and Naomi Griffiths's article "Acadians in Exile: the Experiences of the Acadians in the British Seaports" (1974), published in *Acadiensis*, volume 4, number 1.

Chapter Six: Joseph

To build an idea of what Acadian life would have been like before the Expulsion on what we now call Prince Edward Island, I relied heavily on Earle Lockerby's *Deportation of the Prince Edward Island Acadians* (2008). From this work, I was able to track down sources like De la Roque's census and some letters Father Jacques Girard had written regarding the conditions Acadian families faced on the island.

Chapter Seven: Marie and Josette

A brief mention in a letter by the infamous spy Thomas Pichon— pointed out to me by Stephen A. White and reproduced in a copy of John Clarence and Alice de Kessler Lusk Webster's *The Life of Thomas Pichon: The Spy of Beausejour* (1937) —was the key piece of information for this chapter. I was able to trace Marie's family's path to the Saint John River Valley, where, as church records document, several of her children later married. The rest of the background material on the Acadian Exodus to French territory, and the efforts of the resistance to push back against British movement in the area, was sourced from Sieur de la Roque's 1752 census of Acadia, excerpts from Pichon's autobiography contained within *The Life of Thomas Pichon: The Spy of Beausejour*, and many secondary sources.

Little is known of what life was like for the Acadians who, like Josette, fled to Île Royale between 1750 and 1758. Sieur de la Roque also compiled a census of the island in 1752, which includes sparse details on family names, professions, and the size of communities. Fortunately, he also included where most families came from and how many years they had been in the colony.

To reconstruct the battle at Louisbourg, I relied on information gathered during multiple visits to the fortress, now a national historic site, material from the already mentioned Francis Parkman's *Montcalm and Wolfe*, and several secondary sources, including Richard Hough's *Captain James Cook: A Biography* (1995), where I found passages from the *Pembroke*'s logbook. The guides and employees at the fortress were wonderful and entertaining resources. Apparently, many Québécois and Acadian visitors spit on the floor before leaving the reconstruction of Augustin de Boschenry de Drucourt's residence — an expression of disapproval of his decision to surrender the fortress in 1758.

Chapter Eight: Marguerite

Earle Lockerby's fantastic work "The Deportation of the Acadians from Ile St.-Jean, 1758" (1998) published in *Acadiensis*, volume 27, number 2, and his citations and bibliography, were invaluable to hunt down the sources I needed to write this chapter. To create a picture of what happened when Rollo arrived on the island, I made use of letters sent between Rollo, Amherst, and Boscawen, found in *The Journal of Jeffery Amherst*, as well as excerpts from *The Journal of Admiral Edward Boscawen* and *The Journal of the Hind*, written by Captain Robert Bond, master of the warship *Hind*. These sources are located in the Records of the Admiralty, Naval Forces, Royal Marines, Coastguard, and related bodies, found at the National Archives of England.

To reconstruct the voyage of the *Duke William* and the fate of several of the other transports in her company, I relied on George Winslow Barrington's *Remarkable Voyages and Shipwrecks* (1880) and several other records, including a letter Father Jacques Girard sent to Abbé de L'Isle-Dieu, Québec's vicar general in Paris; a letter Captain Nichols wrote, published by *London Magazine* (December 1758); and "A Remarkable Circumstance Respecting the French Neutrals of the Island of St. John, Related by Capt. Pile of the Ship Achilles," found in the journal *Collections of the Royal Nova Scotia Historical Society Vol. 2* (1881).

Chapter Nine: Cécile

To give an idea of what France was like when Cécile landed in 1763, I relied on Christopher Hodson's *The Acadian Diaspora* (2012) and Oscar William Winzerling's *Acadian Odyssey* (1984). The extensive bibliographies of these two books led me to the primary sources used in this chapter. John Clarence Webster's *The Career of the Abbe Le Loutre in Nova Scotia: With a Translation of His Autobiography* (1933) was also an important source. I relied on Henri Sée's *La France Économique et Sociale Au XVIIIᵉ Siècle* (1927), translated by Edwin H. Zeydel, to depict life for the impoverished in France.

Chapter Ten: Survival

To tell the story of the Louisiana settlement, I again referred to the *The Acadian Diaspora* by Christopher Hodson and *Acadian Odyssey* by Oscar William Winzerling as starting points. Cajun historians have created a wealth of material on the Louisiana settlement, and I owe them a debt, most importantly for the work of Carl A. Brasseaux, in particular *Scattered to the Wind: Dispersal and Wanderings of the Acadians, 1755-1809* (1991).